Introduction

As I introduce this information, which is as old as time itself, I hope to set a new platform for those who will read and open their minds to some light that may emanate from it—the mothers, fathers, uncles, aunts, grandparents, and especially the youths of today, who will become the adults of tomorrow if they don't die in their ignorance first. I wrote this book to both connect and challenge the mind to open new ideas of thinking, and especially for our youths to have a new meaning of life itself.

In applying myself in understanding the scripture, my heart sank within me, as I was faced with purposeful light that placed me under a microscope, forcing my mind to examine myself—a panoramic view, one might say, of my life. It humbled me. I see a love that is beyond my understanding of Paul's statements in Romans 7:18 (KJV), "For I know that in me (that is the flesh) dwells no good thing: for to will is present with me; but how to perform that which is good I find not," and Romans 7:21–23 (KJV), "So I find then a law, that when I would do good, evil is present with me. For I delight in the law of God after the inward man: But I see another law in my members, warring against the law of my mind, and bringing me into captivity to the law of sin which is in my members."

Which of us cannot plead guilty to this? With one hand, we outstretch with kindness. But with the same hand, we kill, for we are intoxicated with the love of a man called pride and with pride. Self presents itself, and the love of God becomes blurred and sometimes lost altogether, putting all together and fornication becomes our cherished child.

We have a god that is infinite in His mercy to us, His creation, and beyond anything we can ever imagine or comprehend. I AM the I AM. Can we ever wrap our minds around this statement? It is a resounding *no*, so we stretch the imagination as far as it will take us and we build idols for ourselves to quench our thirst, which lead us to live outside the boundary of what His guidelines permit.

This triune God, whom we have so many names to describe, has created a place called Earth for us, His creation, to live and thrive. The Word says He visited us for He came down in the cool of the day to speak with His creation Adam (Gen. 3:8, KJV). He did not take Adam up in heaven; He came down to Earth. My belief is that He made planet Earth for the human race—not the black, brown, red, white, or yellow race but the human race. We have created a division to the human race for our own selfish motives. This has created chaos and strife within the human race over decades of time.

In this book, I elaborate expressly on the physical sexual acts and how this is used to dishonor God in the same way as how we use the spiritual mind to dishonor Him. I am sure that many reading this book will say I am just a disgruntled woman. I am fine with this, for there is no way all that I say will appeal to everyone, for one man's garbage is another one's honor. This has been the case for quite some time, so I am not bothered in the least. This is not written to coerce or force anyone into change—but as a reasonable, functioning individual, isn't it time to truly reason within oneself if the Word of God is a lie? For we all have the same beginning and the same end (life and death). There is no doubt that people are searching for meaning in their lives. We only have to open our eyes and watch programs like Oprah's interviews (in OWN), with many questions on spirituality and life and also the many books on life after death. There is a hunger that cannot be quenched by the material things we achieve through the works of our hands. There is a longing, a thirst that is deeper than those things that we once hold dear.

There was a time when I believed that the people of my time in history was so horrible and wicked and those in the Bible was so good and beyond reproach, but a closer look led me to realize that they were no different than who we are now in this time of history. They were faced with the same obstacles, if not more, as we are today because of greed and bigotry. We are dealing with the same evil powers that the Bible has opened up to us. They had the same lawlessness, the working poor, the homeless, the blind, and such. We just seem to have heaped upon ourselves more diseases of the mind and body as time goes on. We are blinded by the same luxury we have attained through usury sometimes (an example is the crash of 2008). This may come as a surprise to many, but we all have a yearning for love. It is not the love of our families, friends, colleagues, or spouse but one that goes above and beyond we can ever call emotional. We were born with it. We were created with it, and we cannot get away from it. Some may say a murderer or a rapist or those who do some of the most heinous crimes have no love, but I beg to differ. It is there, but through freedom of choice, they made a choice to go in another direction. We use the word *mental cases* to cover many crimes.

On planet Earth, there is a fight for life, for we are not just dealing with a fight of the sexes but we are also in a fight for the *mind*.

The craziness I have come to understand is that we are all participants in doing wrong. None is exempt, even those who are theologians and have studied the gospel stories and have read the Bible from cover to cover have entertained and willingly accepted to do wrong. I see myself in every youth, whether an introvert or an extrovert or one with a filthy mouth or lips of sweetness. It doesn't matter. At one time or the other, we were at a time of rebellion. From birth to the grave, we are going to follow through in action to someone; it's a chain reaction to follow in the footsteps of someone because we are relational beings.

We are relational beings because Christ Jesus or God the Creator (whichever one may believe fitting to use) is a relational being. The Word of God states, "Build me a Sanctuary that I may dwell." The question asked is "dwell where?" And the answer returned is among and within His creation, the people made for worship. He who knows all and knows mankind eventually would need a physical structure outside of themselves to believe in, so a physical structure was instructed to be made as a sanctuary carried around everywhere His people went at one time. At this time in history, we now know the physical structure is the people, not a building made with wood or stone. This is where He dwells.

The chain reaction begins as we communicate and share thoughts with one another and share secrets at times, whether rational or irrational. Regardless, we share them.

The human race was created for a great destiny, from the time of conception in which our journey began, whether we live or die within or outside the womb. For this book, I will stick closer to outside the womb.

Through one's lifetime, we make a string of relationships. Many relationships will bring us to the brink of disaster, like a car heading over a cliff, breaking through a guardrail. Sometimes the guardrail will miraculously prevent a death, or sometimes it will not, depending on how determined that individual wants to end his or her life. I say this loosely for many youths, if asked the question, "Would you willingly end your life today?" They will say no or look at you, as if they have lost their minds. But in essence, their lifestyle is pushing the guardrail to end their lives prematurely, and they don't know if it's the youth who goes joyriding with their friend(s) after getting a new car or if it's the one who starts taking drugs because it's cool to do so. Hollywood has not made it any easier with sex, booze, and drugs.

Many choose to believe the Word of God is just a set of false doctrines laid out over time to control the masses, and society says "Do your own thing. It is okay." This is the biggest one of all. Everyone believes in a higher power, but many do not believe in a man called Jesus, who is coming to this planet called Earth, stating He is God in the flesh and has authority to rule all flesh. Some are still looking and waiting for a Messiah. This is how corrupt the minds of men are. Hypocrites! If one can believe in such a being that is all-powerful and without border, why is it so hard to believe this being can do anything, even becoming flesh to be physically seen by man's eyes? But if the eyes and minds of our youth can be so saturated with material things and the feel-good syndrome, they will never be able to change this world for the good or the betterment of mankind, and that is the agenda perpetrated by those creating confusion to keep strife well and good.

I would rather know a man/woman who does not believe in anything (just be a blank slate) than to say they believe in God but not Jesus. Our youths of today are faced with this dilemma every day, for we have so many types of religious thoughts out there. Again I say, how can one believe in a being that spans the existence of time, space, and matter and not believe that being who can (or for those who is having a problem of personality) manifest Himself into a human form. They are liars (plain and simple).

The truth of the matter is that there are those of us who have set up an agenda of who lives and who dies in poverty of the mind, not of food and water. Our youths are being born every day under this umbrella, so they become rebellious—not necessarily because they want to but because they feel they have to in order to survive. This is the reason why Darwin can write of the survival of the fittest, for every day the eyes of our youths open to a new day, with the survival mode kicking in. *Do I want to get out of bed? Should I brush my teeth? Is Mom and Dad going to stay together or get a divorce? Should I go to school? Should I go to church? Should I make friends? Should I vent? Will I eat today?* Should I, should I, should I, or will I—and the list gets longer and longer. From this "should I" and "will I" list comes Mr. Disease, which we name bipolar, anxiety, aggression, or depression.

We have a growing generation of mental illnesses. This is a system in which our youths are born to spiritual death. The awakening of their God-given spiritual minds have been so bombarded by so much stuff that it is hard-pressed to rise above the slops built into our societies. They have no recourse but to fornicate impurely each and every day because they are in a survival mode.

Some may ask the question, how can they when some of our youths are born into riches? But I say they are even more at a disadvantage because they have more opportunity to learn and seek out the truth than those who are in a more unfortunate situation, yet they have joined the bandwagon of their parents' legacy of riches and glory, which convolute the mind. I will not excuse myself to also say they are just as prone to the same illness of Mr. Bipolar, aggression, depression, and anxiety as the unfortunate. What do the unfortunate and the so-called fortunate have in common? They have impure thoughts, which lead to impure deeds—fornication. The Word of God has been put on the back burner, pretty much like where we put it on the back of our one-dollar bill. It is interesting that the percentage of the rich is so small compared to the poor and disadvantaged, yet the Word of God still says there is no lack. It is either the Word of God is a lie or there is a lie perpetrated by another. There is something wrong with this picture. Our youths are slaves to the bondage of greed and bigotry. I am sure if the question was asked of our youths, what are two things they would rush to have in their lifetime among many other things, and it would be success and money because they have bought into the lies that this brings happiness and contentment. What they do not see or understand is that these same folks who profess to this on the outside are dying on the inside because there is no peace. There are those who perpetrated the lie that since we are people from different backgrounds and countries and have our own way of worship, there should not be prayers in schools, yet we are all supposed to be following the same principle of peace toward one another and to worship the Almighty. The fact that prayers are taken out of our schools, they have kicked the Almighty out through the door, and everything else can now enter—from how to use a condom or baby mama dramas. Everything has gone to hell in a basket for the guardrail is removed. It is now fair game—open season. Hunting season has begun. What are our youths to do? For many, homelife is a wreck and school life is no better.

In writing this book, I came upon the prayer of Pastor Joe Wright—which he read on January 23, 1996, in which he was asked to open the session before the Kansas State Legislature—which I have requested and was granted permission to print. Pastor Joe Wright, in short, simple words, completely sums up this whole book that I wrote, as there was nothing that could be added or taken away. It says it all. It sums up the distastefulness of our societies. If such simple and Godly words could have created such a stir among so many, both national and international, what would happen if our youths in one voice would turn to the one and only living God? What marvelous things would happen to the societies of the world? But until then, we can only pray for the mercy of God to continue restraining the hand of the evil until the time of reckoning when He who made us says "no more."

Rabbi Cahn, who spoke at the fourth annual Washington—A Man of Prayer event held at the US Capitol, gave another powerful message for the nation on April 29, 2015. I will not print his message here as everyone has an iPhone or a laptop (look it up). The warning is clear: God is speaking, but the people are sleeping. Kingdoms have come, and kingdoms have fallen. America is no different. What God has given can be easily taken away. King Solomon prayed after the temple dedicated to God was built, and God heard his requests and answered. But when the people turned away from the Almighty, destruction came, and the temple that they clung to did not save them, for God was no longer there. The restraint was lifted, and the people were left to their demise. It took five hundred (some say eight hundred) years for Rome to fall, and it did fall.

If one wants to know if there is truly a system for the failure of our youths, one need not look too far or read every book, article, or column to see this reasoning. Just take a look around your neighborhood. Just look at simple things, such as why there are so many liquor stores in certain neighborhoods versus others that are more affluent. Why is it that drugs seem to pour into less desirable neighborhoods versus affluent ones? What message is being conveyed here? Many, if not most, of our youths are living in these neighborhoods, struggling to make it out[1]. Like I said before, if the mind is messed up, it is easier to be enslaved to wrongdoing. They are more prone to injustices of the land of their birth.

My husband found it funny to see the expression on my face as I count the amount of liquor stores in our small neighborhood—not that he approves of the amount but it is easy to tease me because he knows where I stand in terms of this sort of things. It is easy to keep one ignorant and stupid to what's happening around them, for if they are oblivious to the facts, it is easy to control them; so keep them happy and in a fog with a bottle. So we buy bottle after bottle of booze to keep us ignorant and happy—and not only ourselves as adults but our youths too, for these liquors are left exposed in cabinets and tables for easy access so they can become intoxicated, happy, and foolish too.

Now someone may say "Where is fornication in this?" The answer is, it is right at your door, knocking. Here comes wisdom: "Wine is a mocker, strong drink is raging: and whosoever is deceived thereby is not wise" (Prov. 20:1). Why are we putting the belt to our children or locking them away, bringing judgment and punishment to them, when we have withdrawn the most precious thing from our children—the basic, unadulterated truth of living morally right from the light given us through the Word of God? It is a sad case of hypocrisy when we have such bright and intelligent children ready to adapt and learn, and all society has done is fill these vessels with immorality, darkening the light that should shine through them.

I have read in *Time* magazine of January 30, 2017, that the president of the United States made this statement: "I've spent my entire life and business looking for untapped potentials in projects and people all over the world, and that is what I want for our country." If a human man, so fragile, can say this, what about a God who is also trying to break through that untapped energy that our youths harness or possess to know Him?

Now we have a group of ever-growing young people that is willing to defy all odds to do their own thing to early death or jail, for this is their attitude. "It is about me and no one else." Worse now, the selfie is a new implementation; even our president is in on this one.

Many of us want to separate ourselves from the lesser desirables, the ones whose language is a little hard on the ears or just their presence is too much to bear. But I tell you, when disaster and calamity hits, status does not matter. It will be every man's soul that will be at stake. Fornication is at its height in our world.

---

[1]   **Condoleezza Rice on her interview on PBS Newshour:** *Today, the sad fact is that, for the children who have the fewest options, the educational system is not delivering. If I can look at your zip code and I can tell whether you're going to get a good education, we've got a real problem.* www.pbs.org/newshour//bb/education

In writing this book, I have become more convinced of several things:

1. As long as there are human beings inhabiting this planet, we will have trouble.
2. We are very selfish beings, and nothing can tame that evil within us except the Word of God.
3. No one is ever going to be truly safe for the threat of domination is always going to be present, because man is never satisfied. It has been from the beginning and will be through the end.
4. The only way to have true contentment is in and through the Word of God.
5. Human time is moving quickly.
6. Things within time are very transient; nothing stays the same (here today, gone tomorrow) except for those things God put in place—the sun and moon (celestial bodies).
7. A man called Christ Jesus was born in the flesh. He lived in the flesh and died in the flesh to give us a firm foundation of how to live and how to love according to the will of the Everlasting Father.
8. Through His death, we were redeemed.
9. The belief in the promise that He will return again in the future to this planet to gather a group of persons who hold to this promise and faith.
10. We are all equal in the sight of the Almighty (one true God).
11. War was never God's intention for planet Earth, but due to man's rebellion against God's principles, this planet became a battleground.
12. It was never the intention for human beings to live a life void of His spirit, only to be born, amass as much wealth as they can, and die.
13. The churches are filled with fear due to emotional, verbal, physical, and sexual abuse.
14. We are victims of our generation, which in turn create victims of ourselves.
15. Not everyone who professes to be man/woman of God was sent by God.
16. Everyone comes to the revelation of truth at different time during their journey.
17. Men and women are designed differently for different purposes.
18. Like Paul, until we all can come to the realization that all things gained should be counted as a loss when it comes to the understanding and knowledge of Christ, nothing else matters, we are just playing Russian roulette with our lives, waiting for the next bullet.
19. Many will come and go and draw men away from the true knowledge of God.

20. To know God and to begin to have a relationship with Him is to understand ourselves in the scheme of things, our daily lives, and our individual journey—who are we, why were we created, and where are we going?
21. Deception from many churches appears as light and not deception.
22. Never be too quick to judge or come to a conclusion of anyone until you can walk even a mile in their shoes. State a fact if you can, and in time it will reveal itself.
23. Many may feel that the Bible is fictional, written by man for domination. But I believe even with insertion of scribes here and there centuries ago and with so many bibles written, for the most part, it is an inspired book of instructions given by the Almighty Himself, written for our good, not for pain but for enlightenment even in these dark days.

May God's blessings be everyone who is willing to read and understand with an open mind the gravity of the time we are living in and choose this day to decide who they will serve—God or man.

An Eye Opener to Some Truth of Fornication within the Young Generation

This is an interpretation of fornication from one viewpoint of a woman. What is fornication? According to the *Webster* dictionary, *fornication* typically refers to "consensual sexual intercourse between two people not married to each other." The Bible also places it in the same context of *idolatry*, "a devotion or worshipping." For most people, both old and young, if you ask this question, What is fornication? they will quickly answer that it is a sexual act between two unmarried persons. And it ends there. The thought will never more than likely enter their minds about anything else for that matter. The thought would never occur to them to imagine the spiritual decay in our society when we go against the law of God.

We accept more things in nature in a carnal sense than spiritual, and we expect our children to have morality and values in their thinking. The Spirit of God is always going to be the basis of who we are, and nothing else is important. The Universal Creator to which we are indebted has said time and time again that He is a jealous god and will not take second place in our lives, even though we have placed Him second place every day in our lives with our lust and desires. Anyone or anything that touches His Spirit (the essence of who we are) that is against His will is offensive to Him. What we give up so easily and freely in ignorance touches the spirit of our Creator. Each time we invoke the spiritual side of ourselves, we touch the Creator (our one and only God).

It is almost impossible to honor our Creator in an unholy union between a man and a woman, where there is no blending of the Holy Spirit between those two individuals, likewise so it is with the blending of the spirit with the Creator. He (Almighty God) wants a relationship that is grounded and rooted in Him in love, and we cannot do this unless we acknowledge Him by faith, giving ourselves freely to Him. Ephesians 3:17–19 (KJV) states, "That Christ may dwell in your hearts by faith, that ye, being rooted and grounded in love, may be able to comprehend with all saints what is the breath, length and depth and height and

1

to know the love of Christ which passeth knowledge, that ye might be filled with all the fullness of [Him] God." Look at the importance of who we are to Him (does this seem familiar as when we are together with our loved one?). Ephesians 4:4–5 states, "One body, one Spirit, one hope, one Lord, one faith one baptism," (how interesting) to immerse and to dedicate oneself. Isn't this what we are doing when we give ourselves to another? Christ does not mix words about how He feels about us. He (Almighty God) is loving, sweet, clean, just, and righteous. He is the lover who watches closely. Look at how Jesus, who cares deeply for His own, educates us as a lover.

First, He educates us on areas of our bodies to be aware of (our mouth) because He knows that our mouth gets us into so much trouble in speaking, seducing, or otherwise. Ephesians 4:15 (KJV) states, "But speaking the truth in love; may grow up into Him in all things which is the head, even Christ." Isn't this what we all want from our loved ones? He doesn't leave us in the dark; He tells us what the consequences are for doing otherwise, describing those "who being past feeling, have given themselves over unto lasciviousness, to work all uncleanness with greediness" (Eph. 4:19, KJV). He is not in the business of control. He (Almighty God) will not coerce us or force us in any way to do anything because He gives us free will to do it or not to do it. We can walk in the dignity of right decisions and also learn the consequences of our wrong decision. Free will is the greatest love of God. It cannot be any other way because He is the embodiment of love. This is the reason why He manifested Himself in human flesh to show this to us. Christ has allowed us to experience that darkness to help us realize the pain that goes along with hurting one another through the words we speak. Words bring deception, and many a heart is broken through them, so He alerts us to the speaking tongue/mouth.

For many of us, it takes a long time to repair that breach, whether it was a longtime, close friendship or a person we confided in at that moment. For each hurt and pain we go through, it touches the essence of our Father, as each of us is the embodiment of Him. There is a hymn that I sing often, "Does God feel our pain? / Oh yes, He does. / Does He feel when I'm hurting? / Oh yes, He does." For a time, I couldn't understand what it meant to sing this song, for all I know, it is just me who feels the pain and no one else for how can someone else feel the pain that I am feeling? We have this old saying, "How can you feel my pain unless you walk in my shoe? Do not pacify me with your understanding until you can walk in my shoe, for you do not know what I'm going through." And that is partly true for in each of us, we carry the memory of pain because we are the embodiment of something greater than us; it's spiritual. The spirit within each of us groans when we face devastation in our lives.

Fornication in terms of a sensual act, in my opinion, is the oldest problem faced by human beings from the beginning right down to this day and age. Man

2

has inherited a past that he must fight against: for thousands of years, mankind has made love according to a certain pattern that has become recorded in our cells, and it is very difficult to erase this pattern (Omraam Mikhaël Aïvanhov, *Sexual Force*, 29). Nowadays, young people demand sexual freedom, thinking that it is the road to happiness and fulfillment. Little do they know that by giving themselves to pleasure, they are sacrificing their most precious godly energy. Morality has broken down to the point that our youths of today have no concept of truth. Sexual promiscuity begins early. Studies show that from 40 to 50 percent of US teens are sexually active, with 20 percent having sexual intercourse by age fifteen.

Young people ages fifteen to twenty-four account for nearly half of the nation's nineteen million new sexually transmitted infections each year. With so many showing disregard for God's instruction regarding sex and marriage, it's no surprise that the nation is suffering from curses of abortion and illegitimacy (*The Good News, World News and Prophecy*, January-February 2013, 5). The generation of today believes in what feels good, "what I can get right now and everything goes" syndrome, and they do not care what they have to do or who they need to attack in order to get what they think they need. In speaking to most of our youths, they feel frustrated and betrayed. And because they lack the understanding of how to truly handle these emotions coming from themselves and others, they become involved in youth gangs and the media (BET and other such stations), where anything and everything goes on some of their programs. From this entertainment (if one can call it as such), youths are exposed to women being demoralized through videos, movies, and music that is played against the backdrop of these movies or videos. As if this situation is not bad enough, there are video shops where one can go and play violent video games, and these games are played out in many schools, in streets, and in the homes. Most people, however, play games in their homes or other people's homes. Our youths are technologically overloaded. The young minds are constantly kept active due to technology (social media) in texting, Facebook, Twitter, linked, blogs, u-tune, Pinterest, and other sites and the newest one, selfie. In terms of TV shows, we don't have to look too far as we have the *Family Guy* and *The Simpsons* portraying one of the most obnoxious sibling characters (Bart Simpson) in a family who has no regard for family or foe, which follow through with a father who is just the same. An article written by Stephanie Pappas (Live Science senior writer) on March 28, 2011, states that today's kids face "Facebook depression," in which it states, "From sexting to 'Facebook depression,' the online world brings up a host of issues for children and teens, according to a report released today (March 28) by the American Academy of Pediatrics (AAP)."

The report recommends that pediatricians talk to their patients and their patients' parents about cyber safety, including privacy, anonymity, and cyberbullying.

I recently had an experience while waiting for a bus going home in which a woman started a conversation with me, stating that it is ridiculous how wired in people are to their iPhones. She stated that she was trying to catch one of the trains but was confused as to the one she was to take. She tried asking some of the persons next to her, but they were so busy listening to their iPhones that she had to go to several persons to have her question answered.

She went on to say that if there was a fire and she screamed "fire," most of them there would not hear. This is how much we are wired in to technology. It's not just adults but also babies who are not able to speak audibly for clear understanding is now entrenched into this technology, as I have witnessed. Science has made claim that technology has played a role in our lives, as our skills in critical thinking and analysis have declined. I remember before the electronic cash register went live in the supermarkets, youths who had these jobs as part-time cashiers had to check change. Now if there is a discrepancy at the cash register, they are lost as their brain cannot seem to process in calculating the correct change. Technology is great in so many ways as it increases the imagination and gives us a glimpse into the future of man's capability. Through technology, man has gained much insight of what seems impossible to become possible. The statement or claim in the Word of God is sure that whatever man thinks, he will do. Due to technology, the Word of God can now reach people in some of the remote parts of the world, changing lives for the better, one person at a time. Doctors are able to use robots during surgery and to examine internal organs on a video monitor to guide the surgeon. It is also sad to say that negative things also come by way of technology, such as violence shown in video games, desensitizing real-life violence. This is why it is so vital for mankind to be so nourished in the principles of the Word of God.

Many parents in the past placed more emphasis on using the television as the main source of entertainment for their little ones, but now these entertainments are expanded to video games on the Internet, cell phones, DVDs, and others. I have watched a mother trying desperately to separate her teenage child from his cell phone during a church service. The youth had no interest in what was being said as he continued to play his game on his phone, disregarding his mother's constant touch. Our children are overwired. They eat, sleep, dream, walk, and talk because of technology. This is their world; this is their environment. This is where they are most comfortable. They are the ones changing the world for better or for worse, depending on how one views the use of technology. If they could defy gravity and bring this world to a screeching halt, they would.

A big chunk of kids' social development now takes place in the online world, according to the report. A study released in February 2010 found that 70 percent of wired American teens and young adults use social networking sites. A 2009 poll conducted by Common Sense Media found that more than half of teens use a social networking site more than once a day. The issues that come up—bullying, sexual experimentation, interactions with strangers—aren't new, O'Keeffe said. But the Internet adds a twist: Bullying becomes cyberbullying, teens *experiment sexually* by sexting (sending explicit text messages or photos), and interactions with others are colored by anonymity. In some cases, *sexts-gone-viral* have led to child pornography charges being filed against kids who forward on the explicit photos.

The *New York Times* reported on Sunday (March 27) about one such case in Washington state. The three teens charged in that case later made a deal to amend the charges to a misdemeanor—telephone harassment. Parents and pediatricians have begun to report Facebook depression, in which a teen becomes anxious and moody after spending a lot of time on the popular social networking site. Author Gwenn Schurgin O'Keeffe of the AAP's council on communications and media said, "Technology acts as a great amplifier. Navigating the online world has its share of pitfalls." Kids and teens can inadvertently make embarrassing information or photos public—bad news for future college or job applications. "Sexts" can go viral. Cyberbullying can mean a kid never gets respite from the cruelty of peers. According to the Pew Research Center, one in six children, age twelve to seventeen, receives a sexually suggestive nude or nearly nude picture or video of someone they know. Our youths are overwhelmed by sexuality.

I have no problem with online activities, but when they are not beneficial with good things entering in the minds of our youths, there is a problem. It's everywhere—while they are walking, driving, on the bus, on the train, or riding a bicycle. You name it; it is there. The mind is overwhelmed with so many things that there is no space for God / Universal Creator. Our children are on edge. They are on a supernatural highway, always in readiness for a fight, an argument to the slightest thing that they may deem problematic. Someone profits financially, while the population of youthful minds are like zombies waiting to explode.

Changing Characteristic

> In childhood and youth, the character is most impressible. The power of self-control should then be acquired. More than any natural endowment, the habits established in early years decide whether a man will be victorious or vanquished in the battle of life. (*The Desires of Ages*, 69)

I dare not say it is an easy task in raising children especially in this time. There is no one glove that fits all; however, the Creator assigned this task to us, and we are to bear this burden and carry it through. For those who do not have biological children, there are no excuses. They are also in the business as those who bear children because the results of who these children will become will certainly affect everyone sooner or later. Where they will sit will depend on what has been fostered in them—senators, governors, theologians, presidents, prime ministers, teachers, robbers, thieves, murderers, or homeless. If one watches their child carefully, certain characteristics will start emerging. How many times have we said or heard others say you are just like your father, mother, or someone they know? Why do we say these things? Obviously, it is because we are seeing an emerging characteristic coming from this child that was possibly inherited from the family. I am not speaking of those characteristics that are benign, the temporary ones that will soon fall away, such as following friends in playing pranks on others or speaking or dressing just to become accepted. I am speaking of those that are deeply rooted, surfacing from deep within. If parents are carefully looking, they will observe these traits in their children. Our children are adapting even quicker to things and ideas than children born ten or twenty years ago.

One of my daughters working in a day care told me that she noticed that the babies who were in her care would start crying at a certain time of the evening, and it always happened at the time their parents came to get them. At first, she did not pay much attention to them as she tried to calm them down. But as time went on, it became apparent to her when her child—who was in another day care—was doing the same thing. He would start crying just before she got there. She was told by the aide who was in charge of her son. What is this saying since these babies cannot read a clock? How would they know when it's time to be picked up without seeing their parent(s)? Did God place an internal clock in each of us with the capabilities for time? And if so, what are we doing with the time given to us while we are alive? So as my daughter can notice these characteristic changes, it would stand to believe that we can start very early to speak Christ Jesus into our children at an early age. We as grown adults—mothers, fathers, aunts, uncles, grandparents, sisters, brothers, nephews, cousins—can stamp the Word of God into our children from an early age. It is nothing for a child to be strapped with a bomb and go out to kill without blinking an eye. And if so, why can't we stamp the Word of God into our youths to stand up boldly in these times of so much trouble? Why are we seeing so many youths being indoctrinated with militant ideology as their lack of understanding and emotional overflow take charge, propelling them to harm others? It takes time to prepare oneself to commit a crime, whether it's a robbery or a murder. And during that time, the focus is steady. These youths kill innocent people. But in fact, they are innocent victims themselves, infuriated by what they see and open to those who perpetrate violence, while many of us sit back within churches, not heeding the warning to educate our youths (build them up) not with smooth things but with the true Word of God to build a defense against the infiltration of this ideology to hurt and kill. Today those denominations seek friendship with the world. They preach a message designed to soothe the emotions and win popularity contests. They don't preach about the *cross* of Christ or the blood of Christ because that would make people uncomfortable.

So the people who go to those churches no longer hear the gospel—they hear a message of feel-good platitudes designed only to keep the pews warm and the loose change jingling in the collection plates. Today too many of us had our visions dimmed and our comprehension clouded (Pastor Michael Youssef). This is a dismal truth, but this is where we are. Majority of us have locked up heaven to ourselves and, in return, lock it up also for our children, as we rush for success and money.

We are noticing more and more youths are committing some of the most shocking crimes. During investigations where persons interview youths who commit these serious crimes, you will more than likely hear statements made up, such as "he or she was such a quiet boy/girl/child," "never caused any trouble," or "we don't know what happened." Is it possible that the signs were there, but no one was paying attention, especially those in the home? How many times have people said, "If I could go back, I would change so many things." I know I have. I have gone to my mother about things that affected me in my younger, growing-up years to ask for an explanation. How did she miss so many things about me that I asked? My sister and I speak a lot on the subject of why she changed course early in her life and why I started midway in mine. My mother's answer was she was still learning and thought she was doing the right things for her children. I am sure if she asked her mother, she would probably get the same answer.

In our family, all firstborn girls were given the same name: Evelyn. But for me, I broke the link and changed the name of my first daughter. I wanted to change the tradition of that name (Evelyn). Is it possible that I thought changing the name of my daughter would change her character? My daughter is very happy with the name I selected. Many of us do see these character changes but ignore them to growing pains, and they will soon grow out of it, and so it is left alone. Others will see the changes and try to approach it reasonably with a parent, and it sometimes felt as intrusive to that parent, so the situation is left alone. Many will see the changes but are too afraid to say or do anything because of negative retaliation from some parents or even the youth themselves. One has to remember—this fight is not ours alone but God's. It is He who made the requirement of procreation, not us. As the author Omraam Mikhaël Aïvanhov mentioned, "What is the good of believing in God if your faith produces no result, if it does not transform you?" (*The Book of Divine Magic*, 66) Do what is right, and leave the rest to God.

What character are we building in our youths? They are the building blocks of tomorrow. If our children are not taught from an early age how to see and believe God's light, believe me, there are those who are willing and able to teach and show them the opposite. When children are not taught spiritual matters before leaving home, whether for schools or otherwise, they are easily able to be taught otherwise. There are those who use the power of thought to influence athletes taking part in sporting competitions, and many have triumph by these influences. "Man's lower nature is always there, ready to manifest itself and urge him to exploit every means he can get his hands on." This is why several races of mankind have already disappear from the face of the earth, and our own will meet the same fate if love and kindness, the moral dimension, are not given priority.

"Left to itself, the intellect has no sense of right or wrong, and this means that, when it is given the upper hand, its only concern is to put more and more highly sophisticated technical and scientific means at man's disposal" (*The Book of Divine Magic*, 11). The author said "left to itself." That statement alone lets us know that the Almighty God could not leave us alone to raise ourselves, so it would stand to reason that some form of guidance had to be set in place, and this is what we call the Holy Bible. If we had no other book in the world to read except the Bible, we could live a wonderful life. More and more, as I have said before, we are hearing of these gruesome crimes committed by our youths. And the word being given is mental issues. Many of our youths are killing parents, others, and themselves. As Omraam Mikhaël Aïvanhov said, "Left to itself, the intellect has no sense of right and wrong." Recently, a young man, Nehemiah Griego, fifteen years old, killed his parents and siblings and showed no remorse as he texted his dead mother's picture to his twelve-year-old girlfriend. And later they both spent the day together. At the end of the day, they went to church together, where he confessed the evil he had done. Interesting! Why the church? Why not go home? One has to wonder, *What went wrong?*

Churchgoing Youths

Many of our youths in churches are more in sync with what's going on in the streets than truly what God is all about. Church is a place of social gathering, like going to a party. And God forbid, if you were to ask them why God dislikes fornication, they will give answers such as because it is bad or it is not pure and God is pure. And God forbid, if they are sexually active, then they already feel defeated of ever reaching out to the Creator, so they disconnect themselves because in their minds, they cannot connect. Thinking about it, they are mostly right because they have not been taught how to truly connect in the first place. We ask ourselves the question, How do we connect with today's youth? because we are all in this together, not to continually pass the buck, playing the blaming game. We are here to pull one another up and show love at the same time.

In God's eyes, we are his little children working together and helping one another, but somehow we seem to have forgotten that innocent stage of needing one another. We forget the trusting bond we are supposed to share among one another. We are not here to tear each other down but to build each other up.

How can we make God real without alienating them? How do we connect the dots (so to speak) in truth without taking away from God's words of Love? Many of our youths, as I have stated before, are already exposed (and raw) to so much out there that they are on the attack and are not readily open to listening. I remember singing a song long ago as a child in which the chorus was "real, real, He is so real to me, / I love Him because He gives me the victory. / Many people doubt Him, but I can't do without Him. / That is why I love Him so, / He is so real to me." I learned this song in church as I swing from side to side among others enjoying the moment. Did I truly understood what I sang, or did it sound good to me? Thinking back, I would say it sounded good to me. I still love that song, but now I sing it with such emotion because it means so much more than life to me. Why? Because it holds a special place in my heart, and I understand a lot more now than I did before. Did I necessarily have to go through so much in life to be where I am now? I don't necessarily think so, though some would say yes. Some would say God needed you to go through those trials to be stronger, and I would say God wants His people to have common sense to know when the beast is at the door and when to close it or get a gun and shoot it (spiritually, that is). I beg to differ. When one so young is not protected by those who should be there to protect them, it is a crime.

The Word of God is there to guide and give wisdom, but many hide behind it for dear life to hide their inadequacy, finding excuses not to do what is right. If any youth is reading this book, listen and listen clearly, *find a Bible* and start reading. Google what you don't understand. Every Tom, Dick, and Harry out there these days has a phone, so if you don't own a computer or a laptop, use your phone. But read, read, read, and do it with an open mind. Don't get me wrong; there are some wonderful teachings and teachers out there but know for yourselves. Don't be fooled by the ministries who put you in a tier system for different amounts of money you donate—fifty dollars will get you so much verses and one hundred dollars and above will get you or the ones who will add your name to a special list for prayers. Ask yourself, *Why is that list any different from the one who cannot give or only gave a few dollars?* As for the prayer cloth and other trinkets I won't mention, *do not* contribute good, hard-earned money for these things. These things have come down to us through history from tradition through the Roman Catholic Church. Christ said He is the one and only way to salvation, and no prayer cloth or trinket is going to get us there.

As one watches these various ministries on TV, more and more time one sees these things being offered. You are putting your faith through these things, believing that through them, you will be healed, prosperous, or otherwise. *Do not do it.* Bibles are cheap, and they make sense. If you don't believe, put it to the test. I have a wonderful and God-fearing friend who purchased a glass object through the TBN program, and she brought it to Bible class and showed it to me. She was glowing over this trinket as she went on to explain that there was something else they were advertising that she was saving to get. I wondered about this situation. All too often, we see churches giving such things as prayer shawls, handkerchiefs, and such delights. All too often, the Bible is used as a whipping switch for someone's agenda. But if our youths are not reading, they will continue down the same road as their predecessors and ignorance will continue to prevail.

Like I said before, fornication begins in the minds of people, not things. If you believe it, you will do it. It's an insertion of things into the brain, and it feels good. And when it's over, many times death is the outcome of that person. It's like a sexual act without any commitment, and what results is a lifeless person. We are hearing truth mixed with error many times in preaching, but how would one know which is error and which is truth, as we swallow all as truth because of the way it is packaged and rattled off to us? The Bible states that in the times of ignorance, God winks, but it went on to state that *now* He commands that all men repent. Does this statement sound like we need to stay in ignorance? I dare say no, but how will we change if we never learn to open our minds and read? What does repent mean to our youths when even a simple word as *sorry* is sometimes hard to get out of them? How will we know that a divorce is brewing when all we know is the quote given to us from the Bible, "Women, submit yourself to your husband," without knowing the rest of the quote? So many is stuck in abusive marriages or relationships because of this quote, and what results is the battle of the sexes.

I remember in my early teen (probably around seventeen years) hearing my mother making this statement, "I hate men." And I remember my response to that was "Mom, you do not hate men. What you hate are their behavior." Little did I know that later in life, I would almost claim the same statement as my mother, as I went through my trials with male figures represented in my life. I came to realize the frustrations that came with relationships. Then I realized something more precious than gold, and it was the Bible. I started viewing my brothers and sisters through a different lens. This brings on a different growth and pain. Now I have an idea of the pain of our savior, Christ Jesus. I feel the bittersweet of human nature.

I also remember my first husband and I asked for help in which we sat with a priest at a church close to our home. The priest spoke with us briefly and gave us a set of questionnaires to fill in, and we were told the answer we seek would be ready in two weeks. We returned in two weeks to get the report. As we sat with him, the first words he uttered were "God can take the impossible and change it to the possible." I already knew that, but how that was going to happen was what I needed to know. The conversation ended there. We were sent home with the report, and that was that. What I left with was more defeat than anything else, and my marriage just hit rock bottom eventually.

Every youth must understand that every man/woman, who claims the definition of a pastor, a bishop, or a priest of God, is not necessarily sent by God, for the Word of God already tells us that evil is wrapped in a shadow of light, which means they sound good, but what they do is a different story. Many goes out calling on the name of the Lord, but God did not send them. Jeremiah 27:15 states, "For I have not sent them, saith the Lord, yet they prophesy a lie in my name; that I might drive you out, and that ye might perish."

Dr. Michael Youssef wrote in his book *The Barbarians Are Here* (which they are already here) the "contaminated Christianity" in which he stated that a number of church movements and fads have emphasized practices not found in scripture. Some people, on both the political Left and the political Right, have contaminated the Christian faith with contemporary political ideologies, and he has given various examples of these thoughts. One of the most potent points he made was on intrigue. We love intrigue, and it does something to us and in us, just as what happened to Eve before Adam followed suit. He wrote, "We love uncertainty, ambiguity, and doubt." Where are our young in this respect? It's the intrigued, uncertainty, and doubt that gets them wound up. If something so simple as the true gospel is spoken, something has to be wrong because there is no intrigue, uncertainty, and doubt. A man named Christ Jesus came and died for sinners (US) to redeem us back to Himself, and before He came and after He left, we are left with instructions on how to live and be safe. It's a simple message. But someone comes along with the charisma and eloquence of words with intrigue, placing uncertainty and doubt in the minds of our young, which is an untapped open field ready for the feeding. And as Dr. Youssef said, a large segment of the evangelical world has become seduced by the world spirit of this present age. And more than that, we can expect the *future* to be a further disaster if the evangelical world does not take a stand for biblical truth and morality in the full spectrum of life. "For the evangelical accommodation to the world of our age represents the last barrier against the breakdown of our culture."

So who is he speaking of and who is the future of this land but our youths? Don't forget, it was not the multitude of persons who left Egypt (except for Joshua and Caleb) who made it into the promised land but the children of them who died out in the wilderness. God's Words have to be heeded if we are to make it and see through the smoke screen set up by the evil one. It is sad to say, but so many of our young who is open to the gospel message, and at the end of the day, are left more confused than when they were outside of the church. I recently had a discussion with a young man who told me that he does not believe the Bible stories; neither does he believe in Satan. He believes people just need to be obedient and humble, yet he still attends church religiously each and every weekend. He feels if he practices humility and talk to people about Jesus, he is good. Is something wrong with this picture?

Question of Sexuality

I believe the question of sexuality outside of the home should be first and foremost addressed in the church. I say this for one main reason, a large portion of time for many of us is spent in the churches doing many things inside and outside for the church. I believe the very reason why so many sexual misconducts happen in the churches is because no one wants to face the facts that it is happening, and instead of revealing them, there is more whispering and gossips than anything. Our youths who are in these churches know of this and look at their elders as hypocrites even though they may not say so to their faces, but to their friends, they do. As a matter of fact, they are more observant than many of the adults in the churches. In fact, what we as adults don't seem to understand is that we are better teachers in showing them about sexual misconducts in the churches than anyone else. Many of our youths are already sexually active or thinking about it, but churches are far too busy working on the next project in bringing in money and making new converts in the church, which, in many cases, those converts are worse off than when they were outside of the church. How did Jesus address this? Matthew 23:15 (KJV) states, "Woe unto you, Scribes and Pharisees, hypocrites! for you compass sea and land to make one proselyte, and when he is made, you make him twofold more the child of hell than yourselves."

In continuance on this, for most churches, there are more females than there are males. Many are sometimes young, single mothers or tired, betrayed, and battered women in general, who are looking for spiritual nourishment. Many times they are the ones who fall prey to sexual predators from within and outside the church. It's as if there is a vulnerability to females in the church. In my youth, I used to hear such talk as "if you want a good wife, go to the church," as if women are on a chopping block to test and prod as to who is best for the picking. I have seen in my life, growing up, so many wonderful women who have been hurt in the church because of lack of understanding, and so they are abused in many ways. These abuses of our youth are happening all over the world in our churches from both small and large countries or from large prestigious churches to small churches. None is beyond this situation. An example is Jamaica (small country), with the headlines: Moravian Pastor in Sex Scandal.

These are comments from the public. "When you want to do whatever you like and want an excuse to do so, call yourself a pastor or a Christian." Most people in this country just use Christianity as a way to cover criminality, and because a majority of the population is undereducated, they just let themselves get manipulated and used. Another said, "In truth a population ripe to be fooled now, past, and later." One even quoted a line from Karl Marx, "Religion is an opiate for the masses." Some are like "Cult, not to mention, it's always the pastors who enjoy the life of luxury, while the members are waiting for eternal life in heaven!" Another commented, "There is obviously a 'white gown' of silence within the church. Are we to believe them next when they speak to us about morality?" If these are the sayings, what are our youths to think? Last but not least is the comment "Time to stop revering the church." I am not here to pass blame but to present the facts of the implications against the perpetrator and the mind-set of the public's views. What are we speaking on intoxication of immorality *fornication* in its highest order.

Sexual overtone is everywhere within the churches; one need not look too far. Example is the dress code. The style of dressing for many of our youths are no different than the celebrities in the magazines they read or movies they watch. One example of this is the style of shoes Lady Gaga is famous for, very high heels, which forces the body forward, putting stress on the muscles in the back and throwing the hips out of place, creating possible problems to the uterus.

Another example is the Stella Awards shown on TV, in particular, the dress code of many of the female singers. These events emphasize emotionally stirring music often accompanied by sensually dressed singers and dancers (Hebrew-Streams.org, "The Female Spirit in Christianity"). The hems of the dresses are most times too high, and the fabric is so closely clad to the body and leaves nothing to the imagination, which would imply a problem for comfortability in sitting and other movements. I repeat, the sexual overtone is everywhere.

The necklines are so low it leaves nothing to the imagination, but that's alright because it is not hurting anybody, so they say. Yes, the Lord says come as you are, but he didn't expect one to stay as they are. He expects growth in moderation. How do we expect to have children of high integrity and morals when we see these things and don't address them in our churches?

The Marriage Bed

Is it enough to say to our youth to let sex wait until after marriage when there are so many who are saying "let's test the water to know if we are compatible before marriage"? The answer is yes. It is still wise to ask our youths to wait until after marriage, for God's Word does not change and never will, especially in this matter. God already knew how He made the human body and knew the ramification of infusing spirits. He knows the boundary of the human body, for He is the one who sets all things in place. And when we cross those boundaries, we start treading on dangerous grounds. Today the tone that is set is "love him and leave him" or "let's try it out and see how far we can go." There is hardly any more covenant marriage. It is the mind-set of "if it works, it works; if not, another will do." It's next! There is no partnership; there is no work.

Even when we see unmarried young ladies with multiple children in our churches, it doesn't dawn on many of the churches to include this as a special area of concern. Instead we have gossiping and bad-mouthing within the congregation. The high integrity and morals, which the churches should hold, is a faceless shamble to the youths who have lost trust. For many who claim to be Christians, they seem to have a distaste for God's moral laws, as they shy away from it. For those youths who are truly interested in doing well and following some kind of rule, they are turned off by the hypocrisy they soon find in churches. They sit and listen to great sermons. But then they are told to get special prayers, and they have to give extra money to get on a special list. But for the youth who are truly thinking, they will say, "Isn't that the same system why Christ beat the merchants and money changers out of the temple? And if they go a little further, they will find out that the priests were getting their kickbacks from those selling sheep and doves to the people in the temple.

Group Home Scenarios

I have worked in several group homes for young men and women, and deep down, they want love so badly, but they rather fight the system. The system is going to fail them most of the time, and for the few who makes it through, it was a struggle. The percentage is few and far between. I met two young ladies several years ago, as I was going through the process of taking classes through the social services division located in La Plata, Maryland, to become a foster parent. In the last week of the classes, the group was introduced to other foster parents and the children they adopted. Two foster families brought their older foster children to speak on what it was like for them being placed in foster care. They spoke of their struggles and how they coped, but in the end, they went to college. One young lady was still in college, and the other young lady had a child, was working, and was looking to get married. They were very happy with their progress coming through the system. I am sure there are others that have made it through, but unfortunately for many, they have a desire to hate everything and everybody. I have worked in homes with youths such as these where there is an energy of destruction. It is unfortunate to say the least that there is the wolf and the sheep personality. How can we avail information to them where it will make a striking difference?

I remember working in a girls' group home, and one of the greatest challenges was keeping the house secured at nights.

There were times when I had to call 911 because there were young males in the house let in by the girls by way of the windows to the bedrooms, which were located on the top level of the house. Or they would find a way to try and distract the aides while allowing young males to come in through the front door. Sex was always the main focus. There was one young lady who would disappear for days at a time and would be found in front of a motel, where she would have been left.

In the boys' group home, there was more of an emphasis of watching sexual movies; however, the focus was the same. One thing both group homes had in common was they found great pleasure in being on the phone (whether it was their own or the group home's) and turning in at nights at the same time. Both groups want to stay up late at nights to watch TV or to communicate on the phone. Fortunately for me, there were one or two kids who were willing and able to have a logical conversation with—those wanted to leave the group home, attend college, and become respectable citizens. However, due to peer pressure in the home with other teens, it was not so easy for them. While working in these group homes, there was no inspiration of going to church. As a matter of fact, the last group home I worked in, which happened to be a boys' group home, there was a church next to the home, which I was happy about, and encouraged the boys to go. While my intention was a good one, several of the boys were not pleased as they plunder and steal from the church. It is sad for as these young male and females aged out of the child welfare system and a stable family is not found for them, they end up on the streets. I met one such young lady while working at a group home. She was homeless and lived on the street with several others. It was so interesting to me that she turned herself in to social services because she was pregnant, and she told me that it was because she wanted to do right for the child she was carrying in terms of nutrition and other aid. Does this seem like a reasonable, thinking individual? As I have said before, they are out there. And if given the right information to grow, they will be healthy, knowledgeable human beings ready to use the Word of God to help others. My hope is to one day meet this young man again.

Church Groups

How can we go a little further to break down the barrier of ignorance in helping the government, the schools, and the churches to help families? One of the things that I have noticed, over several years, is the erecting of larger and larger churches called megachurches. Some churches do need to expand because the congregation has gotten too large for the space they occupy, but for some, it seems that it is all about being like other surrounding churches that is larger in capacity. For those who get caught up in following the crowd, they should remember the demise of the Israelites when they request a king to be like the other groups around them. Expanding a church should be for the good of the people in expanding God's Word and love. Then and only then should this be done because otherwise, this endeavor can be very expensive and can become a burden to the congregation. Expansion of any church should include spacing for the youth of where they can socialize under supervision and be taken off the streets. There should be volunteer services given from within the congregation to groom these young minds for the Creator, and that include sexual matters.

Among the many scandals that came out in recent years, we have seen how youths/children have been abused by church leaders and others, such as the most recent outrage of a Mormon parishioner who was killed by one of his initiates. It was a vast outcry from the nation to know that these perpetrators had so much access to so many youths while acting as if they were doing what was in the best interest of the children/youths. Our youths are like lambs to the slaughter because they lack true knowledge. They do not understand that when the body is abused in this sexual manner, it affects the very core of who we are in Christ Jesus. Something is awakened in our being that can either make or break us going into the future.

In most of our churches, we have different ministries, food, nursing homes, shelters, women, deacons and deaconesses, youths, and such. But how many of these ministries are exposed to their neighborhood teens to go out with supporting chaperones to pray for their teen brethrens? How many go to visit places such as

St. Jude Children's Research Hospital, Shriners Hospitals for Children, children's hospitals, shelters for the homeless, centers for pregnant teens, juvenile centers, jails, nursing homes, and homes for the elderly? It is shocking, just about none.

Usually some of these activities are taken up by the older folks in the church. Is it possible that some of these atrocities could be avoided if the scope of youth activities were broaden? It is not enough to just believe in God if His character does not come alive in you. If I was to tell many of our youths that God is alive and well in them, they would look at me like I have lost my mind and would want to run as far away from me as their feet can take them, and I could not blame them. For as much as there are so many churches and so much preaching happening, it's like speaking a foreign language to them in equating the message of loving Jesus and loving self in the same human body. It would definitely be like speaking a foreign language. Churches are filled with persons with different qualifications, such as doctors, lawyers, accountants, and such. Why is there not enough teaching or seminars done for the youths, especially in respect to the inner workings of the body? The church leaves such wide openings due to their inaction to enjoin God's Words and belief to God's little ones. The gate is left wide open for other doctrines to come in and take a stand.

There are youth camps through several churches, such as the Jimmy Swaggart Ministry, Seventh-day Adventist, and the Potters group (T. D. Jakes) to name a few. It's wonderful to see the bright, young faces shining and hungry for the Word of God. These young minds return to their respective home churches refreshed and filled with what they have learned. I am sure they leave with such anxiety to spread the good news that Jesus died for us all and sin is in the world. Thank God the light is turned on.

The Genie Is Out of the Bottle

If we think things are bad now, there is a bigger fight now for the minds of our youths as we now have what is called the After School Satan Club, whose goal is to place an After School Satan Club in every school where there is a Good News Club or any other proselytizing religious groups that have established a presence. According to the Satan's club emphasis, a religion need not make exclusive claim to a value, ethical principle, or practice to advocate its advance. My god, where is the guardrail?

The battle still rages and will continue until the most benevolent, supreme master of the universe appears. Our youth have a choice to make.

Where Is the Government in This?

Another enemy of our youths is government cutbacks, which affects well-needed, affordable programs in the communities. Numerous studies show that children born into fatherless homes are far more likely to die in infancy, to be poor, to show aggressive behavior, to abuse drugs, to have behavioral problems in school, and to spend time in jail or prison. The social and economic costs of teen pregnancy and childbearing are often high, and these costs can be both immediate and long term for teen parents and their children. For example, teen pregnancy and childbirth contribute significantly to dropout rates among high school girls. Only about 50 percent of teen mothers receive a high school diploma by age twenty-two compared with nearly 90 percent of women who did give birth during adolescence. Teen pregnancy and childbirth cost US taxpayers an estimated nine billion dollars per year because of increased health-care and foster-care costs, increased incarceration rates among the children of teen parents, and lost tax revenue from teen mothers, who earn less money because they have less education (CDC's teen pregnancy website, http://www.cdc.gov/teenpregnancy).

In the 2011 fiscal year, federal and state governments spent a combined $450 billion on assistance to low-income families with children—with about three quarters of this or some $330 billion going to single-parent families. This average is out to about $30,000 in assistance to each single-parent household (*The Good News, World News and Prophecy*, January-February 2013, 6). Due to this situation, it wreaks havoc on families who are barely trying to keep their heads above ground to keep food on the table for their families, so parents are working two and three jobs, which leave youths with little or no supervision.

There was a time when you could find youths in the grocery store bagging groceries, but even that has been taken away as we turn more and more to technology, so here is another area where youth has more time on their hands. This in turn leaves youths to the whim of negative devices and advice from the wrong persons. The governmental system is broken. In September 2012, the total deficit passed sixteen trillion dollars—an amount exceeding the nation's entire GDP. And as shocking as these figures are, they in fact vastly underestimate the scope of the problem. The United States is experiencing a drastic turnaround unparalleled in history. The bottom line is America's cities are broke, and the nation is broke (*The Good News, World News and Prophecy*). In a few weeks, another president will be inaugurated, and much will be spent for the festivities. Some of us will be doing just about anything to buy a ticket to go to the inauguration ball. Martin Luther's birthday is coming up shortly also, and projects will be in place for this event. Can a tenth go to the effort of helping the situation with the youths?

Where Are We in All This?

There are children as young as eight years old outside of their homes at late hours of the night with little or no supervision of parents. Most of these neighborhoods have a church in the vicinity and sometimes multiple churches, and I sometimes wonder where the shepherds are. Are we praying enough for our communities? Are we going above and beyond to reach out to our neighbors, who may need our help, especially those with young children?

There is a situation that recently came to my attention, and it truly touches my heart. This was the plea of a mother asking for help from her community in helping to remove what she considered hostile, young men idle on her street each day. She has children and is concerned for their safety. She took it upon herself to speak to the men of her concern, but they paid no attention to her. Her plea went out, and the comments came rolling in. One person said she should seek help from her neighborhood church even though they may just shrug their shoulder at her. This is a dismal case of how many view the church. The comment made as to the church turning a blind eye to a family in distress saddens the heart. What are our youths growing up in these neighborhoods to think of this God who we belong and honor? These are some of the things that start fornication in the heart from a young age. This is not only about the government but about all of us coming together one accord. What happens with our youths today affects all at some time or the other. In some neighborhoods, there is what we call neighborhood watch, where residents take turns to make sure no one breaks in to our houses and steal, plunder, or do any other damage. If we can protect that which can be replaced, what of our children? Our youths need a wake-up call. Where is the curfew, which was once set in place?

Young people are always in such a hurry for experiences that will rob them of their youthful freshness, their zest for life, and even their health. And they are not content to burn their fingers once; they keep repeating the experience over and over and over again until there is nothing left of them but a heap of cinders.

And they go to swell the numbers of those who keep doctors, psychiatrists, and analysts fully employed.

First, they want to experience every pleasure and every kind of excitement however dangerous. In fact, it is diametrically opposed to your tastes, for it is the nature of human beings to be eager for novelty and adventures, which gives them a sense of greater intensity in their lives (Omraam Mikhaël Aïvanhov, *Youth: Creators of the Future*, 56 and 58).

Children are having sex in school bathrooms. Young ladies are dressed in uniforms with their lips painted and hairdos, which seem to appear that they are going to a place other than middle or high school. I remember a time when students dressed modestly and are checked before entering into classrooms for clean hands, no makeup and certain apparel.

Now these things are accepted as creativity. I do not write of the lipsticks on young girls or the long hoop earrings in their ears going to school for a parent(s) to get in an uproar and negatively confront their child but as a pointer that you are seeing visible signs displayed. This is a wake-up call, for if you haven't started speaking to your youths as yet, it is now time to do that because they are alerting you that they are transcending to a different spiritual level of growth.

Even their change of friends and the places they hang out is sending a message. If parents do not know how to approach the subject matter, pray about it (nothing beats prayers) and have the Spirit of God lead you to someone or a book. There are many parenting books on the market. If money is an issue, check your local library. Don't forget, these children are wrestling with their own changes also. The Bible states we are born in sin and shaped in iniquity. They don't know. I listen to two friends speaking on the bus in which one young lady said that she took what sounds like a preparatory exam. It was not her but a friend who took it for her, and she found nothing wrong with that. She only knew that the exam scored big marks under her name, and she was very happy about it. Her friend went on to say that she was finally able to get her own Facebook page, and she was surprised at the amount of followers she had and people who called her. Now she can put all that she wants and say all that she wants. They have not a clue of what they are doing. I have asked my children to be very careful to what they put on Facebook, which includes exposing themselves and my grandchildren in such manner as to draw negative influences to themselves and their children.

I had an experience in 2005 while visiting a church of a very close friend, an elderly woman who I had come to love and admired deeply (still do). As a matter of fact, she came into my life from a referral of a friend, as I desperately tried to find a good sitter for my five-month-old daughter. In meeting her, immediately my spirit was drawn to her, and I felt a comfort level with her that I called her my second mother. She was one of a kind. I wished every mother could find a sitter like her. I happen to visit her church on a Sunday because one of her friends, who was living with me at the time, needed a ride to church, so I took her. I decided to stay for the service and take her back home. On that Sunday, they had a visiting pastor doing the sermon. During his sermon, he made several comments about the youths of our time. He told the congregation that if a young man happens to walk into the church and sit down in which his pants was without a belt and below his waist or bottom, he was to be thrown out of the building. I was furious but made no comment until after the service had been adjourned and prayer was said and everyone was leaving the sanctuary. While in the hallway, I spoke to a few of the congregants about his comment, and they had an issue with it also but said nothing. I told them that I had an issue with his comment for my question was "could it be possible that a mother or father have been praying for that son to seek God and change his life, and it just so happen that the prayer was heard and this young man found himself in church that day?" Now what right does anyone have to throw him out? I said the pastor spoke foolishly. Does he know the joy of that father or mother to see that son in church? My concern was taken to the pastor, who did the sermon, and he was very upset at my comment but never confronted me. Several of the young men and women wanted me to continue coming and helping them to change some things there, but I did not feel that was my fight at the time, and I told them to seek God's guidance for change. I have not returned to that church since that day.

I have seen families become estranged from one another because of the situation where the children's growth of change becomes a concern, especially in Christian homes, and one spouse or the other does not know how to handle it. It is war in the home to the death of that marriage. I have known of one such marriage where the father started calling his daughters whores and witches, ungodly children. The fight started, and the marriage ended bitterly with the mother getting the children and the father leaving the home. Both parents also split apart and eventually attended different churches. This was so sad. Only through love and continued prayer for understanding can we combat the fear of influence that is hell-bent on destroying families. We are now seeing on television the episodes of *Preacher's Daughters* further exposing the topic of sexual freedom from teens, which touches just about every family.

As human beings, we are also spiritual beings, but we look at everything in a physical aspect. Our children are not taught spirituality to allow them to understand God's love, and so when it comes to spirituality and sexuality, they are lost. They are taught to understand that one should go to church because it's good to do so, and besides, it is a tradition. The Word of God says, "People perish for lack of knowledge." If Christ is always around us in the form of the Holy Spirit, then wouldn't it make sense that He is a part of our being? When you explain the essence of Christ's death through pain, they understand the spiritual implication as to something emotionally felt but not physically seen. Can they associate this with the hurt deep down after a breakup of a relationship that they thought would last, a trust that was broken, and the list goes on and on and on? If we explain the changes that are taking place in their bodies during this emotional time, they will understand the effect but not chemical changes associated in the body. Tina Turner sang a song titled "What's Love Got to Do With It." Within the song, she uses words such as *must understand, pulse react,* and *a thrill.* She is telling a story of awareness, but what does all this mean to a young woman and a young man? It is not only physical as is claimed, which is in fact logical, but how deep it goes. Is it just physical and not spiritual, for it hits to the core of attraction from one to another? Why is it she chooses the words *must understand* and not *should understand*? It's clear that something happens with a touch that creates a reaction in the body. There is that chemical oxytocin again, which is that feel-good sensation we get.

We can see the physical and spiritual clearly at work here in the song—the spiritual, which is the emotional attraction, and the thrill, which produces a response such as the butterfly sensation in the stomach. Here she tries to explain reasoning in which she says to try to ignore (danger area) and that it means more than that. As the song continues, "That it may seem that there is confusion going on when there is a closeness and she tends to look dazed, / she has read it someplace and have got cause to be" (but somehow, there is a twist in the song and rational thinking kicks in), she decides to take on a new direction in protecting herself because that kind of emotion she experienced was scary. Another song was "Upside down, boy, you turn me inside out." We had better start bringing these things to the church where it really matters because this is where the tire hits the road for our youths. This is where their interest lies. Just the mere fact of where millions of dollars go, buying these labels tells us something to what interest our youths. God embed in us the spirit of awareness, and when we ignore it, consequences are sure to follow. How many of us have found ourselves in this position, and what decision did we make? Did we ignore the danger and plunge right into a relationship with that individual or listen to that soft voice (conscience) that says "stop and think"? God made the body in such a way to be sensitive to His presence, to ward off fear and know how to react to different situations.

Now we can explain why God hates fornication in a deeper sense because it affects the essence (spiritual) of us, which affects God. God is involved in every molecule, every gene, and every strand of our being. And the only way to be released from that bond is through death, which results in the separation of flesh and spirit. Can we love like that without being presumptuous? To separate the two during a living state is pure madness because it is the essence of who we are. If asked, how could this be? Genesis 2:7 states that God formed man and blew breath into his nostril, and man became a living soul. (Can one live without breathing?) They are beginning to get the point. We are realizing now that more illnesses are originated from the cells not getting enough oxygen to sustain vital health—so air is vitally important. It is the daily sustenance for our being.

He is the air that we breathe, the food that we eat (manna from above), and the water we cannot do without (springs of living water—his Word). What was Christ tempted with? The same things He made: food first, a kingdom that already belongs to Him, and then worship. What are we tempted with? It is but the same. Can we pass the test? And can our youths?

Emotion Connection (Sensory Channel)

Can the soul (man) be touched outside of emotion? I don't think so. The soul can only be touched as a reaction from a physical experience—a trauma through death, injury, or excitement (something that impacts the physical body). It can be touched through various avenues—taste, touch, smell, and sight. Can these emotions touch God? I think so, as we are made in His image (Gen. 1:26) and packaged in His Spirit. How do we know emotion touches God? Genesis 2:17 states that God gave a command, "Of the tree of good and evil, do not eat." What happened? The end result was, they ate (disobedience through the taste sense). And our first parents, Adam and Eve, could no longer physically see Him but could only hear Him. Was God hurt? Yes, He was. Did He have to give us this test? Yes, He did, for Christ is a god of bountiful love, and He wants our love to be the same as His, willingly given. The question was still asked, was God hurt? The answer is still yes, He was, for He knew how much that action on our first parents was going to cost. He did not mix words for He said, "Of the day you eat of that tree, you will surely die."

Some would say, "Did they truly understand what the Creator was saying?" The problem was not that they truly understood, as it was obeying a command. The Bible is silent on this point. The Bible said their eyes were opened and they saw that they were naked. You see, what Eve did not seem to understand in totality is that she had everything and what the serpent wanted was just her allegiance (worship). Eve saw what seems to be the appearance of good, something to make one wise, but it was a deception. It makes one think what chemical reaction started as they made the decision to disobey a command. Through that decision, Adam and Eve fornicated, giving allegiance to another, tipping the balance in the favor of another, not our Creator. They invited another into their being. Their innocence was gone. The intimacy with the Savior disappeared, and hardship followed soon after. What Eve did not realize was that in order for Lucifer to have allegiance, he needed separation first, and that could only come by obeying him. Eve had no idea of the cost she was about to unleash upon this planet (Earth). I can just imagine what emotion must have been running through her mind (I can be like God, wow, awesome). Her mind was probably in a swirl, flooded with anticipation of what she can become with the knowledge she would gain through the deception of the snake, forgetting all that the Creator had taught her husband, who, in turn, would have told her about the tree of good and evil.

The temptation of wanting to achieve all that the lying snake was promising was too good to be true and too good to pass up, so she went for it. How many of us have been tested or are being tested by the snake time and time again and says the same thing, "This is too good to be true"? We hear the old cliché "All that glitters is not gold," but we fall for it time and time again by the promise of luxury. One of the greatest ones is "If one will go to school and learn, everything will be open to you"—a great job, luxury, and entertainment, the best life has to offer. Nothing is wrong with having some form of luxury, a great job, or some entertainment. But unfortunately, majority of the time, it is never in moderation. Now, many who read the story of Adam and Eve would call this woman stupid and would throw every negative slug at her for accepting such a thing, but then how many are doing the same thing today? Temptation starts at an early age. "If you do this, you will get this." And how many of us in turn share those same temptations with others—brothers, sisters, friends, colleagues, and God knows who else—so they become partners in crime with us too? We share good as well as bad. The more the better, right? Eve probably did not think she was doing anything terribly wrong. After all, she shared it with her husband, who had more teaching than she did, and he ate also. The Bible states that what they saw looked good to their eyes, but it also states that when we are tempted and fall to it, it is because we are drawn away by our own lust or strong desire. Eve's lust and desire was strong enough to forget the instructions given to them from the Creator. Obviously, they must have thought that He (God) must be hiding something from them that we can be gods just like Him and would never die. We have this saying in our time, "Curiosity kills the cat," and in this case, it killed a whole planet of generation after generation.

Now sin exists because it was welcome a long time ago. Our youths are opening the channel to the evil one daily because they are given to pleasure, power, control, and self-satisfaction. Lucifer could not affect our foreparents (Adam and Eve) as long as they had the light of the Creator around and inside them. He (Lucifer) knew he had to remove it first to gain the right to dominate. He (Lucifer) had to darken their minds with selfishness to gain control. He (Lucifer) knew how precious the human family is to the Creator, and it was out of jealousy that he was thrown out of heaven. And it is his sworn duty not to have us enjoy the connection with the Creator. Unfortunately for him, the all-knowing God already made plans for our salvation because we are spiritual beings, as I have said before, and He knew long before the fall that (we) His children would have fallen. No matter how much we stray, we will always be connected to Him.

In the *Express* 2016 paper of March 3, one of the well-liked celebrities expressed his disgust for the media about rumors but said that he is judged by only one power and he serves him. It would be interesting to know what power he is referencing, but one will hope that it is the infinite one and only universal power (the Almighty God). I believe it will be the youths who will make the revolutionary change and return that homage to the Creator, and they will be coming from the ones who many would never believe to do this. It is the youths who will say "true and righteous are his judgments: for he hath judged the great whore, which did corrupt the earth with her fornication, and hath avenged the blood of his servants at her hand." Many will say, as I said to myself a long time ago, "How could Adam and Eve do such a thing, knowing that they were warned against this enemy?" But I say, "How many of us knowingly give homage to another other than our Creator each day?" Our youths are unknowingly doing this daily, moment by moment, without any regard for the Creator. What is sin? It is the transgression of the Creator's laws. The Creator has given us laws not to punish us but to keep us in harmony with Him and one another. He is the Almighty God who chose us, not the other way around. He is the big brother who comes to our aid when we need Him the most, not the big brother we call on when we want to do evil, as most of us are used to doing. This is why it is so important for us to place a protection edge around them with truth, not misguided information, for Satan knows that it is through these little ones, the human family relies for growth. And Satan hates families. One youth can give birth to several children without a thought of how these children will be fed, will live, will be educated, or otherwise.

Without the proper guidance, Satan has that family in its grasp from cradle to the grave. One of the greatest reasons why Satan hates the human race is he hates everything Christ stands for, which is replicated in us in 2 Corinthians 4:7 (KJV), "But we have this treasure in earthen vessels, that the excellency of the power may be of God, and not of us." Lucifer knows if he alone has worship, this would create chaos to this earth and this world as we know it would cease to exist. This happened twice before, once before creation in Genesis and the second during the time of Noah. If our children are not taught to reverence our Creator through worship of all our senses, then we are bound to repeat the same misery.

School System

For many, it's expected for the schools to train our children to have good etiquette when most, who are teaching our young minds, do not have that principle themselves. Teachers should give far more attention to the physical, mental, and moral influences in our schools. When special attention is given to the thorough development of every physical and moral power, which God has given, then students will not leave schools calling themselves educated while they are ignorant of the knowledge that they must have for practical life and for the fullest development of character (Ellen G. White, *Advice to the Young* vol. 5, 523). Those few who truly care and are in the school system, they are overwhelmed by politics and bigotry, so where does it leaves us as parents? Some cry out to teach them better sex education, while others say that topic should be left at home while the young turn to technology and friends. Some say to turn to technology and block certain channels, and some have no TV at all to protect their children from the world. It is interesting that one voice cries "It's unconstitutional" to have prayer in schools. It was granted by the Supreme Court, the highest court in the land, but then the government gave money to churches and schools for sex education (contraceptives and abortion). Now I do understand the fear for many in terms of prayers as there are so many children coming from different religious backgrounds. This would definitely create a problem; however, the situation of sexuality being taught in schools did not seem to create a problem for those same children in the same situation of diverse backgrounds. Is it an oversight, or that it doesn't matter?

It is still a taboo to speak of sexual things in many homes. Most cry as I had once myself done, "How can I teach what I do not understand?" As the Ethiopian said to Phillip when asked, "Understandest thou what thou readest?" he answered, "How can I, unless someone explains it to me?" (Acts 8:31)

This is not written to blame any one person but to call attention to the threat facing our youths daily, for it is the parents first and then the church who need to speak out on this matter. The more sexuality is hidden, the more curiosity unfolds. Let me ask the question: Is it wrong to start stimulating the minds of our children at an early age in intimacy in a godly way about sexuality?

At what stage of the development do our children become more and more curious about themselves, while most of us are too busy doing other things to even notice the changes taking place? For those parents who does, they sometimes have not a clue where to begin, and so their youth lean to their own friends for understanding, which many times lead to bad results. Every child, at one point or the other, questions their sexuality, whether they are from a broken or an orderly home. The question is where they get those questions answered. It is a natural thing for us to want intimacy. To reiterate, this was instilled in the human race from creation. Sexuality is divine by origin, but as long as a person does not know how to control oneself, the manifestations will clearly not be divine (Omraam Mikhaël Aïvanhov, *Love and Sexuality*, 22). A baby expresses attachment to his/her parent(s) very early in their life from the touch they receive, whether by kisses, hugs, snuggles, voice, or tickles. The response is usually favorable. As children develop, they continue to develop their sensual aptitude (KidsHealth. org). Puberty can be a very confusing time, with lots of physical and emotional changes, and children need to know what to expect in the months and years ahead even if they are too shy to ask. If curiosity or inquisitiveness was never dealt with properly at an early age, then misfortune and missed opportunity are bound to follow. Sensuality is not a misdemeanor; it is right up there with air. It's a must have. We were born with it. It is spiritual; it cannot be erased. The Lord knew what He was doing, and He did it well, so why should you want to mutilate His creation? (pg. 36)

Ellen G. White (founder of Adventism, 1827–1915) wrote that young children should be taught at home until they are at the age of five years and not placed in a classroom in which they should be taught by their parents through nature to understand the basic things while in their innocence. But I do understand that this scenario is not possible, for many, including myself, their children started in a classroom setting at the ages of two and three. Most parents have jobs outside the home; some sometimes have two and three jobs just to make ends meet, and so the children suffer in those early years in getting the nurturing they deserve. Mrs. White said (*Testimonies for the Church* vol. 4) that those who would make a success in the education of the youth must take them as they are, not as they ought to be nor as they will be when they come from under their training. The educator of the youth should feel an unselfish interest for the lambs of the flocks. There is too little pitying tenderness and too much of the unbending dignity of the stern judge. Exact and impartial justice should be given to all, for the cause of Christ demands this, but it should be remembered that firmness and justice have a sister called mercy. Men and women of experience should understand that this is a time of especial danger for the young.

Our children are bombarded from every direction of morality—the television with its sensational records of frauds and embezzlements, of misery in families, husbands eloping with other men's wives and wives with other women's husbands, the TV shows, church scandals (a perfect example is the Hasidic therapist of the Orthodox Jewish community that was sentenced to 103 years for sexual assault), teachers sleeping with children, of promiscuity in other areas, and a host of other things.

I usually choose the TV shows and movies I watch most of the times on Netflix, but at times I watch regular TV shows, flipping through the channels. One such night, while doing this flipping, I decided to watch the TV sitcom *Bones*. To my surprise, one of the leading characters who has a young son was always busy with his work on the job, and his son thought that if his father has a girlfriend to have sex with, he would be able to move in with his girlfriend, or vice versa, into a house that has a pool in the yard. During the show, this young boy tried to get females to be girlfriends of his dad for this reason. He asked one female character if she was sexed up. She told him that at the moment, she is practicing celibacy to which he replied, "What is that?" and she explained. The father who was clearly uneasy about this troubling situation with his son had no clue how to address the idea of sex with his son, who clearly had the wrong idea of sex, but somehow thought that sex was something to do to get something one wants, in his case, it was a pool. One of the leading female characters explained a waiting period and came from a scientific point of view to show complete control over when she had sex and how she chose a mate who knew how to do the job properly without any emotion attached. Another visiting character (a young lady) was having her struggles with when to have sex with her boyfriend, and she was told eventually that she would know when would be the right time to have sex.

Looking at this scenario, how any of our youths thinks of sex as just something they want? How is the message of sex become so twisted? And what message is left to the mind of when to have sex? What does the Word of God state when left to our own thoughts without a sound, solid foundation? Psalm 81:12 states, "So I let them follow their own stubborn desires, living according to their own ideas." "So I gave them over to the stubbornness of their heart, To walk in their own . . . of their own hearts, and the counsels of their own heads." What else did it say? Proverbs 3:5–6 states, "Trust in the LORD with all thine heart; and lean not unto thine own understanding. In all thy ways acknowledge Him, and He shall direct thy paths." Isn't this clear enough? So what is the character in *Bones* implying when she said to the young woman, "Trust yourself, you will know when it is the right time to have sex"? As humans, it is a very conflicting time during this period of young adulthood when sound advice is needed, not left to their own understanding. It sounds so wonderful in these movies when statements like these are made. "Trust yourself. I know you will make the right decision." Well, those "trust yourselves" have led to many miserable lives.

"The youths are becoming educated to a high standard of literary attainment; and sin, unbelief, and infidelity are becoming more bold and defiant, as intellectual knowledge and acuteness are acquired" (Ellen G. White). This sums it up so well. Our youths have no clear understanding of the sanctity of life, so it is easy to kill and to rape without any sense of wrong. The erotic zone of our youths is so stirred up that a young man (youths) can rape a small child without a blink of an eye while his friends watched and videotaped the situation. Is lockup the answer for these youths who has done this terrible deed? And if so, how will this change the nature or attitude of these teens? Who is there to bring the Word of God into their lives to make a change to future abuse?

Recreating the "I AM"

I have oftentimes wondered why the Almighty God said to Moses, "Tell the people when they ask, that I AM the I AM that I AM." The Israelites were already in Egypt four hundred years, and most had adapted to other gods. Yet the Divine said to tell them "I Am sent you," as if they would have recognized the name the I Am. The Most High said we are heirs to the kingdom. We are sons and daughters of the Most High God. As adults, we call upon Him every day and every moment of our existence, yet we do not know Him. If we don't truly know Him, how on earth do we expect our children to know Him? Just as how He expected the children of Israel to recognize His name I AM, it is the same that He expects of us and our children. He has placed the I AM even in our very language. How often do we use the words *I am*? Let's look at some of the ways we use the words *I AM*: I am not going. I am your friend. I am Dr. So-and-So, I am lazy today. I am your friend, your sister, your brother. And the list goes on and on. Our children continue the legacy without knowing the sacredness of I AM.

The Bible quotes, "Who is man that he should be mindful of us?" But he created a species called the human family with unconditional love. He (the Infinite) is complete love and wants love in return. The I AM has been fashioned in each of us, and this is one reason why God says, "Whatsoever man thinketh he will do because He [the Almighty] created everything through thought."

This is also a reason (I believe) why there can be depression following an abortion because of a disconnection with oneself and the severing of the divine through the loss of that human spirit, which was on its way in development. Each time a union of sperm and egg come together, the I AM is recreated again and again. Our youths do not think of this, and so sex is just a way to gain physical pleasure to the body. And what comes next is of no effect. If a child is produced from this pleasure, so what? We can either take the morning-after pill or head to the abortion clinics. If we respected the anatomy of what's between our legs, as God's way of recreation through love, we would think twice of abusing that power He has entrusted to us. There are those who is still looking for the Messiah, not knowing that we reproduce the I AM on a daily basis. We are made in His image to see Him in body, just as we see our family members or friends. For now, we behold Him every time a child is born because it is a miracle time and time again.

We are in awe every time we see a newborn enter the world. It's breathtaking. It's emotional. We can't even define the emotion we feel, much less put it into word because it's beyond word(s). We just know that something stirs within us when we look at a newborn. I believe this is God's divine power at work.

Our youths are taught through the actions and deeds of others that sex is a fair game. This is their stand. "It is my body. I can do what I want with it." But what they do not understand is the responsibility that comes with having that body. Christ says, "My Spirit lives in that body. It is my temple, and what you do with it affects my spirit. It is not one that you are to continue to whore with every day, every second, every minute, and every hour as you do." God is not always going to be polite with His words, and the true harsh reality is that many will die (as many already have died) in their ignorance. The Word of God says every time a man or a woman even looks at another with such desire in their hearts, he/she has already committed adultery.

What does that mean to our youths, especially for those who have not shed that innocence to sleep with anyone? What is this statement implying to them? Sadly, *nothing*! For they do not understand the spiritual implication of this statement, but I can guarantee, without a shadow of a doubt, they will figure it out to a point, still not understanding all but that something went wrong when they enter into that role and feel the anguish or pain when things don't work out the way they expect it to. The Word says, "So as a man/woman thinketh so he will do" (Prov. 23:7) or "Out of the abundance of the heart the mouth speak" (Matt. 12:34). What does this mean to our youth? Not much, and I say not much instead of nothing, for this would not take much thinking for them to guess. But in a nutshell, it's going to go through their brain just slightly, and life goes on as usual.

Many times we overlook what a person says in anger because oh, they did not mean it, but is that true? Did the Bible lie? Would one know the truth if that person hadn't blurted out that which has been festering inside for a long time? How many of us are carrying around these troubles like a loaded gun? How about "So as a man thinketh, so he will do." Is that a lie? We have proven that daily, whether good or bad. Man thinks of how to get a bulk of metal to float in the air (we call it a plane) or how to harness electrical current to be used in our everyday lives, but man has also thought up ways to create mass destruction or intentional abuse toward another person. Recently, in the March 31, 2017, *Express* paper, it was printed of an incident between three youths—ages fourteen, seventeen, and eighteen. The paper explained that the girl (fourteen) and boy (seventeen) in question made plans to have sex in the bathroom the next day. Only what the young lady did not realize was the young man thought up a plan to have his friend involved in the action. So when the Bible speaks, "Who can know the mind of man except God and man alone," is this true? Yet our young take no heed to these things because they lack understanding.

I ask the question, is it fair to beat them over the head with scripts of fragments of the Bible when there is no direct link to truly what it mean? My story in this case was the story of innocence not in the sense of age but of mind, for I was well over thirty years of age with two children of my own and was separated from my husband when I encountered a situation in church when an elder in the same church showed interest in me. At times when prayer was said and hands were held, he would scratch the palm of my hand. I had no idea what it meant until a girlfriend told me it was of a sexual nature. Another encounter was with another male in the church who pursued me to the point of letting me know how much he has been trying to get my attention, but I paid him no attention. I was divorced then and saw no problem in having a relationship with him. Why not? We were both of the same religion, and he knew the Bible better than me (or so I thought). I was intrigued because I was so eager to understand the Word of God that we started a relationship. Little did I know, he had a previous relationship of marriage that was never resolved. And when I inquired about it of him, he gave me every excuse of why there was no resolution in that marriage and why he did not see a reason to clean up that situation. The three things I had asked of him were (1) pray about it and repent, (2) contact his wife and ask forgiveness of her, and (3) contact his children and do the same.

During the course of our relationship, which lasted a year, many in the church knew of his situation, but no one bothered to speak to him or me. But God moves in mysterious ways and allowed a guest visitor to our church, who saw and recognized him and happened to make a statement to a dear sister and friend of mind, and she confided in me of what the woman said. Well, needless to say, I ended that relationship with him. God knows those who are truly seeking Him, and He will direct their path. And there are thousands and thousands of our youths out there on this planet Earth that are hurting and in pain and want desperately to know him but don't know how. They are in the most eloquent homes and less desirable neighborhoods, but they are out there.

Dr. Wayne W. Dyer, in his book *The Invisible Force*, wrote, "Reject the concept of 'enemies,' just know that all of us emanate from the same Divine Source." It is that force that gives us the abilities to do anything. It is that force that is invoked at the time of conception before that mother feels that stirring or first kick. It is that force you speak with before that child is born. Many I Am have gone to the grave because we have been given free will. How do we teach our children about the great I Am?

The Womb

Children were given to us for a reason, and that is to extend the worship of the universal creator. The human race was created to populate the earth. The womb was given to females to produce greatness in the recreation of the human race. Within our genetic coding, there is a need to procreate. In Genesis 1:28 (NIV), God blessed them and God said unto them to be fruitful and to multiply and to replenish the earth. (Interesting.) I found the word *replenish* used several times. I might be stretching it a bit, but one would think that there was a race here before. Why would the creator use the word *replenish*? What are we to learn from this word? Is the human race the first on this planet, or were there others here before us? If yes, are we the last? If yes, were they created as we were and born from a womb as we do? Genesis 2:9 states, "In the middle of the garden were the tree of life and the tree of the knowledge of good and evil." For me the symbolism of the geographical location of the tree of life and the tree of good and evil lets me think there is a point to this in terms of man. In the center of man holds the key of mankind, for man cannot be formed without a womb, which is located in the center of the female's body.

fallopian tubes — — ovary

Looking at the surrounding area to the womb, it is fed into by the fallopian tubes and by way of the vagina (should be unchartered territory until needed). The ovaries store the eggs and release them in a timely fashion each month as they make their journey toward and through the fallopian tubes to the uterus. Our Creator is a God of uniformity, order, and functionality. If in the event the egg reaches the uterus and does not find an awaiting sperm to mate, it breaks apart and with it all the preparation and is removed from the body in the form of menstruation. If in the event the egg meets with a viable male sperm, then these two joins together to begin the process of a brand-new human being. God is returning for a group of people well prepared and ready to meet Him with a seal of His characteristic in their hearts and mind, ready to become one with Him as the egg and sperm. There is nothing left to chance—we are made in His image. We are the tree of life to good and evil. John the Baptist said in Matthew 3:8 and 10 (KJV), "Bring forth fruits, meet for repentance and now also the axe is laid unto the root of the tree; therefore every tree which bringeth not forth good fruit is hewn down, and cast into the fire." It is obvious he is speaking of people. How important is it to guard against who we mate ourselves with? Does our youths know or think of this? We equip them with books to educate them to get jobs in the workplace (which is not guaranteed), but the things of which to give them life to its fullest, we ignore.

Much activity takes place in the uterus (womb) to make ready for a new being. It is being nurtured and nourished as the rivers of living water nourish the Garden of Eden. John 7:38 (KJV) states, "He that believe on me, as the scripture hath said, out of his belly shall flow rivers of living water." If one notices, it is not about being dead but being alive. We sing the song "There Is Power in the Blood," and it is rightly so because in the blood is the genetic coding of life. A team of scientists has been able to predict the whole genetic code of a fetus by taking a drop of blood from the mother. The *New York Times* printed, "The accomplishment heralds an era in which parents might find it easier to know the blueprint of a child months before it is born." God's dwelling is in the inner sanctuary (womb) where life is. Each womb is a representation of new life, as God is life. Each child welcomed into the world is for God's glory to profess His truth that He is God and God alone. Each child is a living witness, a living stream that God is real. God knew us from when we were in the womb when we were not even conscious of our being. The psalmist wrote in Psalm 139:13–15 (KJV), "For thou hath possessed my rein: thou hath covered me in my mother's womb. I will praise thee; for I am fearfully and wonderfully made. My substance was not hid from thee, when I was made in secret."

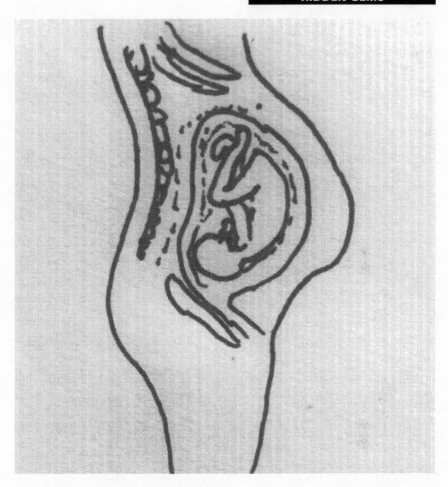

When we think of planet Earth, it has everything man could ever need to sustain life, for it nourishes the life in every sense of the Word from the human, animal, and insect kingdom. There is nothing missing, and when one looks into the female womb, it gives nourishment in every form of nutrient, warmth, and all that's needed to bring that life to fruition.

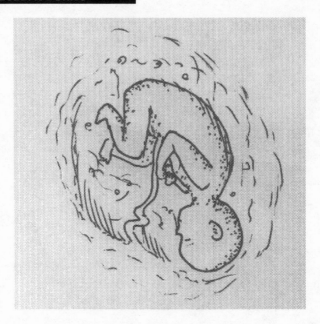

Question: What does it mean that we are fearfully and wonderfully made? (Ps. 139:14)

Answer: Psalm 139:14 declares, "I praise you because I am fearfully and wonderfully made; your works are wonderful, I know that full well." The context of Psalm 139:14 is the incredible nature of our physical bodies. The human body is unique, the most complex organism in the world, and that complexity and uniqueness speak volumes about the mind of its creator. Every aspect of the body, down to the tiniest microscopic cell, reveals that it is fearfully and wonderfully made.

Engineers understand how to design strong but lightweight beams by putting the strong material toward the outside edges of a cross section and filling the inside with lighter, weaker material. This is done because the greatest stress occurs on the surfaces of a structure when handling common bending or tensional stresses. A cross section of a human bone reveals that the strong material is on the outside and the inside is used as a factory for blood cells of various kinds. When you examine a sophisticated SLR camera with its ability to let in more or less light as needed and its ability to focus automatically over a vast range of field, you find repeated imitations of the operation of one of our eyeballs. Yet having two eyeballs, we also have depth perception, giving an athlete the ability to throw a football to a receiver with precision or for us to judge how far away a car is.

The human brain is also an amazing organ, fearfully and wonderfully made. It has the ability to learn, reason, and control so many automatic functions of the body—such as heart rate, blood pressure, breathing—and maintain balance to walk, run, stand, and sit, all while concentrating on something else. Computers can outdo the human brain in raw, calculating power but are primitive when it comes to performing most reasoning tasks. The brain also has an amazing ability to adapt. When people put on glasses that make the world seem upside down, their brains quickly reinterpret the information they are being given to perceive the world as right-side up. Or when people are blindfolded for long periods of time, the vision center of the brain soon begins to be used for other functions. When people move to a house near a railroad, soon the sound of the trains is filtered out by their brains, and they lose conscious thought of them.

When it comes to miniaturization, the human body is also a marvel fearfully and wonderfully made. For instance, information needed for the replication of an entire human body, with every detail covered, is stored in the double-helix DNA strand found in the nucleus of each of the billions of cells in the human body. And a system of information and control is represented by our nervous system, so compact in comparison to man's clumsy inventions of wires and optical cables. Each cell, once called a "simple" cell, as small as it is, is a tiny factory that is not yet fully understood by man. As microscopes become more and more powerful, able to magnify smaller and smaller fields, the infinite vistas of the human cell begin to come into focus.

Consider the single fertilized cell of a newly conceived human life. From that one cell within the womb of his/her mother, develop all the different kinds of tissues, organs, and systems and they all work together at just the right time. Amazing! An example is the hole in the septum between the two ventricles in the heart of the newborn infant that closes up at just the right time to allow for the oxygenation of the blood from the lungs (not used in the womb).

Furthermore, the body's immune system is able to fight off so many enemies and restore itself, from the smallest repair (even down to repairing bad portions of the DNA) to the largest repair (mending of bones and recovery from major accidents). Yes, there are diseases that will eventually overcome the body as we age because of man's fall into sin and the resulting curse, but we have no idea exactly how many times our immune system has saved us from death that would surely have occurred without it.

The functions of the human body are also incredible. The contrast of being able to handle large, heavy objects and yet to be able to carefully manipulate a delicate object without breaking it is also amazing. We can shoot a bow and arrow, repeatedly hitting a distant target; peck away quickly at a computer keyboard without thinking about the keys; crawl; walk; run; twirl around; climb; swim; do somersaults and flips; and perform simple tasks, such as unscrewing a light bulb, brushing our teeth, and lacing up our shoes, again without thinking. Indeed, these are simple things, but man has yet to design and program a robot that is able to perform such a vast range of tasks and motions.

The function of the digestive tract, the liver, and other major organs; the longevity of the heart; the formation and function of nerves and of blood vessels; the function of the lymphatic system; the cleansing of the blood through the kidneys; the ability of the reproductive system to create cells able to mate up with another cell from the opposite gender and produce a cell with twice as many chromosomes; the complexity of the inner and middle ear; the sense of taste and smell; and so many other things we barely understand—each one is a marvel and beyond man's ability to duplicate fully.

Truly, we are fearfully and wonderfully made. How grateful we are to know that God made us through His Son, Jesus Christ, and to marvel not only at His knowledge but also at His love (Ps. 139:17–18, 23–24). (See www.gotquestions.org.)

I found this to be the most awesome, breathtaking explanation of God's handiwork of man's complexity done.

It is unfortunate when a woman feels she has the need to terminate a pregnancy, for each pregnancy that is destroyed for whatever the reason is one life lost to God. A woman, whether married or unmarried, or a young girl who finds herself pregnant has a decision to make. She is now a mother, whether that child lives or not, and I use that word loosely as some may debate this choice of word. We speak of ovum, fetus, but to me I do not negate the fact that if left alone, it is a child that will be produced. I do understand the reason medically for doctors to explain what happens during the process from conception to birth. Our Father in heaven understands interest in knowing what goes on in our bodies as our bodies change to accommodate this new life, but unfortunately for some, this process of a new life brings with it a dilemma of choice—will this fit into my lifestyle, two mouths to feed and educate, a rape or incest situation, what people will think, promiscuity outside of marriage, the father is irresponsible and immature, I'm not capable to love, and the list goes on and on. In this scenario, we see all the reasons for not giving birth, and in this we have a double portion of fornication. As I explained before, fornication starts in the mind first before the act. God is not about negativity but positive thinking, for all things are *possible* through our Lord and Savior. This woman is moving away from godly thinking to her way of thinking. This is fornication on the first level. The act of an abortion completes the process. The Word of God says He knew us from the time we were formed in the belly even from the substance from which we were made. This is what we destroy daily in the abortion clinics here and abroad in the name of love. We are vitally important to our Creator, and our bodies were made to give Him worship. We have taken the right out of the hand of God to fulfill what we believe to be right. We would rather put funds to kill life than funds to expand on ethics and spirituality.

While our youths are rushing to become grown-ups at such an early age, they have no concept of all this, of how precious and wonderful their bodies are. Even in such little example of something falling on our feet, how quickly the hands react to offer help. The Creator thought of everything down to the minute of things. We are so busy in this chaotic life to enjoy what was so tenderly given to us. Some of us have also made every effort in keeping our children busy with football, dancing, piano lessons, and other extra curriculum in the hopes of keeping them out of trouble.

In our everyday "anything goes" lifestyle, our youths suffer. Do they have any concept of all this? I dare not say they do. Too many go to churches where friends are meeting and talking, texting, and making gestures to one another while in the house of God without any respect of what's holy, and we wonder why we have lost sheep. They make no difference or separation between the holy and the unholy. Are we vigilant to the cause of God while we are brethren in the church to the goings-on in plain sight, or are we so closed-minded to what's going on in our own lives? Many preach about Christ, but do they love Him enough to feed His little ones without being vultures in preying on the innocent youths in the church? The Spirit of the living God is at work, seeking and exposing many who have been raping His flocks sexually. Christ asked Peter three times to feed His sheep. Why was it so important that He had to stress this a third time? Obviously, it had to be very important because through each of these little humans, Christ is reborn again and again and again. And He wants the knowledge of Him to be known so that His character can be molded to their minds early before the filth of the world gets stamped there. How they are molded after birth is where the challenge lies.

I have a story of a wonderful friend who found herself in such a situation. Her son had become involved with a young lady, and everyone in their church felt there was something not very right with the relationship. But instead of approaching my friend with their concern(s), everyone kept their mouths shut and spoke behind her back while she struggled with the relationship between her son and his friend. The situation escalated to the point where her son moved out of the house with the young lady even though he knew his mom was against his relationship. I had gone to visit my friend at this time and realized her distress and asked her if she had spoken to anyone in the church about it, and she said no. She had this burden on her own. It had gotten to the point where she stopped speaking to the young lady and was so angry to the point that she would ignore her even while she was in her presence. I was upset with the situation and had gone to the first elder about this issue, only to find out that they were well aware of the situation. When I asked what was being done, he said nothing. I was very upset, and as I stood there speaking to him, I became more angered. He said he understood my anger and said he would have someone come to my friend's house and look into the matter. A few days later, a young elder came to the house and started having Bible study with her son and the young lady. My friend made peace with her son and the young lady, and my friend died six months later from uterine cancer. Her son carried the burden that he had a hand in his mother dying because of the circumstances with him and his girlfriend. His girlfriend was outraged because she was pregnant and had other issues. The young lady—who had such great promise as she was very artistic—went on to have another child with another person and was struggling to make ends meet. This is just one of those examples of the church sleeping during a crisis.

The Lord said His people are scattered all over the hills without a master to guide them (1 Kings 22:17, KJV). There are more and more churches in brick and mortar being built but fewer souls truly being saved. Many go to churches for healing, but they take their baggage to the altar and pick it up again after the service is finished.

Our children are in crisis. I have visited many churches to see many expectant, young, unmarried mothers from early teens to late teens. Where are the prophets/shepherds? It would seem that the mode of the churches are to build bigger (mega) churches and not necessarily better church members, and the members are so proud of these large edifices. It brings to mind the second temple in which the people marveled at its beauty, but as one of the disciples proudly spoke to Christ as he admired the stone in which the temple was built, Christ said there shall not be left one stone upon another that shall not be thrown down. Even into this time, we are still saying, "Lord, look at these great building we have made in your name." Now don't get me wrong because some church buildings are too small to house the congregation and need more space. We spare no expense in erecting these buildings, but Christ is looking for change of hearts and feeding the minds of His people, in this case, the youths.

There are so many in the streets, in group homes, in jails, or in the system one way or another. The field is truly wide, and the workers are truly few. I remember when churchgoing people were recognized as unique and peculiar people; they truly stood out and made a difference in people's lives in a good way. 2 Corinthians 5:17 (KJV) states, "Therefore if any man be in Christ, he is a new creature, old things are passed away; behold all things are become new." 1 Peter 2:9 (KJV) states, "But ye are a chosen generation, a royal priesthood, a holy nation, a peculiar people: that he should show forth the praises of Him who hath called you out of darkness into His marvelous light." They are to be the salt of the earth, but if they lose their flavor, what good are they? For many of our churches today have lost their saltiness, as they resemble the others of the world. For example, we now have joined the pool of reality shows, *The Sisterhood*, which portrays the lives of first ladies of various churches now shown on cable TV. These ladies have now put their lives in the hands of producers and directors, who are not necessarily interested in godly things. Producers are about ratings, and ratings means money. Just how far are these first ladies willing to go to keep the show running? The first time I heard of the show was through a friend at work, and she was astonished at what was being displayed. The next was my daughter who called me up to ask me if I saw the show in which I said no. I am sure these ladies have put some thought into this, but one has to wonder how much soul-searching went into their decision. Some may say times have changed, and there is nothing wrong with this as they are only keeping it real, but where is God in all this? Did He (Almighty God) say to go out there and show all your stuff because you want the world to see and know what's going on behind closed doors? Or did He say to go in your closed closet and pray to your father above and he will reward you openly? Who is in control here? So if you are going through stuff and you need to take matters into your own hands, then you don't need His help. What will make their show any different from any other reality show out there? First ladies, like anyone else, have issues, and they are also human. But coming on television to show a sex object need not be shown to create an atmosphere that they are like everyone else with a sexual appetite with their spouse. If for no one else, I am glad that they are enjoying and immersing themselves to the fullest with their spouses as that is God's blessing. God has given all the ammunition for a healthy sex life. However, coming on television to show objects used in affectionate hour and displaying a banana in explaining how to use a condom is an unacceptable behavior. Our youths are watching, and they may mistakenly take that action as a welcome attraction.

They are already having problems in this department. The line between right and wrong is so thin that when we think that we are doing the right thing, it creates more problems than blessings. This is the reason why the Lord said to search the scripture. Lean not to your own understanding.

In the *Express* paper, February 22, 2013, another of our celebrities announced to *DuJour* magazine that the ninth season of *Keeping Up with the Kardashians* will be her last because her boyfriend (Mr. West) has taught her a lot about privacy. She said that she is a little less open about some things, like her relationships, and I quote, "I'm realizing everyone doesn't need to know everything." (Hello, an enlightenment.) What is it that the youths say? TMI (too much information). I am not here to bad-mouth anyone but only to say we have to be so careful what we put out there when we are representing God on a daily basis. It is not about what the public wants but about how they see the flame of God represented in our lives.

Christ brings everyone in due time and due season, such as this young woman. The love of the Almighty has to be first and beyond in one's life. I am hopefully sure that the intentions of the first ladies are indeed honorable, and they love the Almighty God and want to show they are no different from each of us, who may have passed through some things and have gotten to this time in their lives only because of the grace of God. But when one opens Pandora's box, so to speak, to such a vast audience, one must be careful.

Dreams of Our Children

Our children have dreams that are being formulated from a young age. Little boys usually want to be firemen, and little girls, princesses. As they get a little older and one asks, "What do you want to be when you grow up?" you will get answers such as to be an astronaut, a doctor, a football player, a nurse, a singer, and the like. Usually, by the time they are early teens into late teens, they start to identify with people, such as Tiger Woods, Jay Z, Oprah, Beyonce, Mary J. Blige, Madonna, Britney Spears, the Kardashians, MC Hammer, OMX, Michael Jordan, certain rappers (male and female), football/basketball players, and whoever else is up-and-coming. These are the role models. More than likely, you are not going to hear they want to be like Jesus or the apostles, unless they were brought up in a Christian home and were taught to understand this by parents, grandparents, uncles, and aunts. They are not going to identify with these individuals because they make no true sense to them. Our youths are thirsty, and they are always looking for a new fix because they bore easily, so they are always looking for new faces and new things going on. It's a challenge to keep God's Words alive in them because God is constant, and truth never changes. It's unfortunate that many will get that stage of enlightenment when they are worn, battered, beaten, and off the roller coaster before they seek the Almighty. Their attitude will be focused on vanity (beauty, house, cars) things that can be taken away so easily as the whole duty of man is to serve the Creator.

When one is young, one is inclined to want everything to be easy or to pursue wealth and success in preference to everything else. And then one day, one discovers that the only things really worth acquiring are lucidity, strength of character, patience, purity, and kindness, that it is they that enables us to face up to the unavoidable difficulties of life, whereas without them, even the most resounding success can easily be a disaster (*Youth: Creators of the Future*). Many of our youths follow their idols though their iPads, laptops, and iPhones. They seek fame and fortune, following their dreams through the eyes of many of our celebrities, who show them all the glitters and glamour, especially young celebrities. We only need to look at some of our friend's Facebook page to see how proud we are of our children holding a basketball or football, and immediately, the idea of the NFL and becoming successful is imminent.

Those who try to pursue their dreams to follow through to meet success usually meet exploitation by the hands of unscrupulous people who take advantage of them. Many times what ensues are failure, depression, suicide, or otherwise (*Youth: Creators of the Future*). What our youths don't know are, those idols they follow and praise also have a story line to tell. Some have accommodated themselves and created accommodation with life, and therefore, they consider themselves well-balanced and happy, having all that they want of creature comforts. Yet many of these have lost contact with their souls, and they do not experience God, for they have cut off their soul faculties. And although they consider themselves rich and increased with goods and having no wants whatsoever, they do not know that their souls feel naked and are without anything. There are many who cut off not only their own soul but also their own divine spark, their nonreason for being, and they cut off the angels and God also (Mark and Elizabeth Prophet, *The Masters and Their Retreats*). If one wants to know who our youths are influenced by, just look at their dress codes and also their attitude. As celebrities like Will Smith, Louis Gossett Jr., and Michael Jordan among others start wearing earrings, so does many of our young males. The spark of what makes sense goes right out the window.

Lady Gaga came out with shoes in which the heels are eight inches or more, and one of her styles does not carry a heel, for it is supposedly made in a way in which the female put more emphasis to the front of the foot. Now Lady Gaga does have a problem in walking flat on her feet because of wearing these types of made shoes.

Many other female celebrities have followed in this same pattern. Do they care about the millions of youth whose health is at stake? We have those who have performed in what's called the babylicious pumps while pregnant, wearing these high heels. These things are impressed on the minds of our youths, and our youths in churches wearing these various attires draw attention to themselves in a sexual way with no regard to their body language because it feels good and they find it supposedly sexy. There goes the word again—*sex*(y).

I remember when the series *Roots* aired on TV in 1977. And from that series, many baby girls were born to the name of Kizzi; and little boys named Kunta were born to young people. Our children are very impressionable and desperately need guidance, and if ever they need it, it is now. It is stated in 2 Timothy 4:3 that there will come a time when they will not endure sound doctrine. Is such a time now? The Lord said to Isaiah, "Bind up the testimony and seal up the law among my disciples" (Isa. 8:16). Who was He speaking to? Was it just to the prophets of old? Does it still apply to us today? I believe it still stands for today.

It is said today in the churches that many things written of old was not written for our time, and that is true to some extent, for we do know that Christ went to the cross to die in place of us for our sins. And the sacrifices that were done before are no longer required, but for the most part, the law and testimony still stand to the end of time as we know it. Christ did not give this command to the regular people; He was specific. It was given to the prophets, priests, and pastors, those who are in authority over God's people. Moses was sent from God to release the Israelites from bondage, along with his brother Aaron (a Levite priest), who was already prepared to assist him, for Christ will not leave His people without a representative to represent Him before His people. So it was then, so it will be now, in this case (the youths of this generation), to come to know Him on a personal level. The task of bringing the law and testimony will not be an easy task, as many in the churches do not believe that the law still stands. So this command goes unheeded, and so the message is stifled and does not go forth to the youths.

As the generation grows, we are seeing the climate change more and more as war, chaos, stretches its hands from culture to culture. Youths are taking over. They are changing society daily. One only have to read the paper to see these changes occurring across the land. We sum it up to mental cases when we do not understand the reason for some of the most atrocities done by the youth, but one have to ask, where is the loving God in all this? But I will have to say that we each have to look within to see where we have failed them. We have a generation of youths that is moving further and further away from the Creator, as they lean to their own understanding. This is a dangerous thing, for the Lord always wants to be remembered. This was not only for the people of ancient times but also for the children down through the ages (Deut. 4:9, 6:7; Ps. 78:1–7). If there is no fear in their hearts for God, how much more for you and I. These are the youths who will sit in seats of authority, in seats of government, or otherwise. For those who may end up in politics, what law or laws will they approve? This reminds me of the story of Joseph. After Joseph died, the Word said the pharaoh, who was in authority in Egypt, knew not God and became afraid of the Israelites because of their rapid growth and decided to turn against them. I have included the story of Joseph to say the farther we move away from teaching and understanding using biblical wisdom to control these sexual climates with our youths, the more they will move away from the Creator. Is it possible that the pharaoh in Joseph's time did not come to know Joseph's God because he did not have an experience with the Universal God as his predecessors before him? So will our youths who have no experience with the Creator because their minds are only on a self-made image rather than a spiritual image.

It brings to mind that solemn day on 9/11, September 11, 2001, when there was an attack on the United States ground. I remember the atmosphere of many of our youths on the college ground as they ran back and forth to find the nearest TV room to get information on what was happening. There was so much confusion that it stopped classes that day. Many were in tears because they lost loved ones that day. The religious establishments were full; parking spaces were hard to find. But no sooner as things calmed down, everyone was back to their lives, as if the incident was in a far past. It was one of the saddest moments in history, but one has to ask the question, does a catastrophe have to happen for people to seek God? What are we teaching our youths? That only when they have a need they should try to find Him? Jesus told the story of the people who died in the collapse of the temple of Siloam, and they were doing God's work, yet still they died. But Christ said unless we repent and change our ways, we will also perish, whether we are in church or elsewhere.

Moreover, we have not only youths of the United States born and raised here but from other countries also, who have migrated here with family members, so we have a large population of youth who will be transforming the United States workplace or otherwise, as we are experiencing. History does repeat itself, but as a nation out of pride, greed, and bigotry, many choose selective memory and turn a blind eye to justice, honesty, and integrity. Egypt is repeated again. Isaiah 19:23 states, "In that day shall there be a highway out of Egypt to Assyria." So it also was with Rome—all roads lead to Rome. Now it's the USA. Many have come and will continue to come to join hands with the United States in works and deeds. Many will be called by God to do good works and establish His name and show His mercy, as well as others who will come for other reason. If one thing we know, written by many historians, is that we do not learn from history, so we are bound to repeat the same mistakes. It's like the thief who hears of another thief getting caught and says in his/her mind, *I wouldn't get caught because I would do things differently.*

America the Rescuer

America came to be as a protection for God's people as they fled persecution for justice, integrity, and peace, a place of refuge. But where there is greed, there can be no peace. When will there be a cry, "Go ye, inquire of the Lord for me, and for the people" (2 Kings 22:13, KJV). There is no cry for "none calleth for justice, nor any pleadeth for truth; they trust in vanity, and speak lies; they conceive mischief and bring forth mischief" (Isa. 59:4). America was to be God's vineyard. He called this land a beloved vineyard that he tenderly prepared and provided for a people. What wonderful words! Isaiah 5: 1-2 & 4 (KJV) states, "He fenced it, gathered out the stones and planted it and gave it everything for survival and then he asked the question, what more could He have done that had not done." America has transformed the world in many ways and is continuing to do so. Our latest financial crash has proven this to be true. Its effect touched many countries far and near. We say "In God we trust," but the Lord says in Isaiah 29:13 (KJV), "Wherefore the Lord said, forasmuch as this people draw near to me with their mouth, and with their lips do honor me, but have remove their hearts far from me, and their fear toward me is taught by the precept of men."

A Cry in the Land

I was moved by the prayer of Minister Joe Wright when I read it, for he has taken the mantle to go forth with such offering to our Heavenly Father in such humbleness and forgiveness for our nation, and it is so still right for our time.

Heavenly Father,

We come before you today to ask your forgiveness and seek your direction and guidance.

We know your Word says, "Woe to those who call evil good," but that's exactly what we have done. We have lost our spiritual equilibrium and inverted our values. We confess that we have ridiculed the absolute truth of your Word and called it pluralism.
We have worshipped other Gods and called it multiculturalism.
We have endorsed perversion and called it an alternative lifestyle.
We have exploited the poor and called it the lottery.
We have neglected the needy and called itself preservation.
We have rewarded laziness and called it welfare.
We have killed our unborn and called it choice.
We have shot abortionists and called it justifiable.
We have neglected to discipline our children and called it building self-esteem.
We have abused power and called it political savvy.
We have coveted our neighbor's possessions and called it ambition.
We have polluted the air with profanity and pornography and called it freedom of expression.
We have ridiculed the time-honored values of our forefathers and called it enlightenment.
Search us, O God, and know our hearts today. Try us and see if there be some wicked way in us. Cleanse us from every sin, and set us free.

Guide and bless these men and women who have been sent here by the people of this state and who have been ordained by you to govern this great state. Grant them your wisdom to rule, and may their decisions direct us to the center of your will.

I ask in the name of your Son, the living savior, Jesus Christ.

I bowed my head in tears in reading this testament because this is ever so true. Who am I to speak when I am also so guilty out of ignorance as my brothers and sisters?

The government is burdened by many mouths to feed. There is a loud cry in the country, "Where is the money going?" Millions of dollars are going to contraceptives and abortions. Is the Lord's hand so short that it cannot save, or is His ears so heavy that it cannot hear? No! But our iniquities have separated us from our God, and our sins have hid His face from us.

Our churches say wonderful things, but are they all in one accord? Isaiah 4:1 (KJV) states, "And in that day seven women [church] shall take hold of one man [Christ], saying, we will eat our own bread, and wear our own apparel, [doctrine] only let us be called by thy name, to take away our approach."

America is a very prosperous country, and there is no lacking of the blueprint of life (the Living Word), but for the most part, those who are messengers (pastors, elders, deacons) of Christ for guidance need to be taught again. At a time when those who should be the authority of God's Word should be more vigilant in their work in saving the branches (youths) again, we are once again shaken, frustrated, and thrown off course with splashes over the tabloids and Internet of the immoralities taking place in the churches. What should the young people think? Not forgetting, these are the branches of whom are not grounded or rooted in the faith as yet due to lack of proper foundation, and so the battle rages on as children go against every grain of morality.

Previously, I spoke of the womb with the analogy of the Garden of Eden. In the garden (womb), a place of sanctuary that brings forth life, it is the Lord's. The Lord asked in Isaiah 49:15–16, "Can a woman forget her suckling child that she should not have compassion on the son of her womb? Yea they forget, yet will I not forget thee. Behold, I have graven thee upon the palms of my hand." I believe every child conceived, whatever the result of that child, they are also graven in the palm of His hands.

I remember twenty years ago, one of my dear friends found herself in a crisis after having three children out of wedlock, a struggling mother trying to make ends meet once again found herself pregnant and unwed. She came to me for advice on what she should do. She wanted to end the pregnancy. I agreed with her because like most, I think nothing of it because it was causing so much conflict in her home and being unwed again. Also most of all, it was in the very early stage, so what could be wrong? As she and I went to the clinic on the day of the procedure, God intervened and had the doctor do a sonogram. From the sonogram, which she brought to me in the waiting area, I could see what looked like a heart beating and a formation of a human being. My heart sank, and I told her, "This is on you if you still want to go through with the procedure, but I cannot be a part of this anymore." We both walked out of that clinic that day, never to return, as she said to me, "This baby is your baby, not mine." I guess this brought some comfort to her as she knew the trials she was about to face. This baby is now a teen and the most handsome and talented young man. Each time I see him, I thank God for His intervention. And by the way, my friend got married to his father. In the January 2013 *Reader Express* (in brief), the subject is still being kept in focus that hundreds of antiabortion activists gathered to celebrate last year's decision that a woman is required to have an ultrasound before an abortion.

Chamber of Love

The sexuality (meaning the mind), which was first to be enjoyed with Christ at a young age, is becoming lost to our youths, and they lead a loveless life from cradle to the grave. Isn't this a dismal picture? What could be the cause of this? Ellen G. White wrote in The World Out of Control, page 28, that one reason why many theologians have no clearer understanding of God's word is, they close their eyes to truths that they do not wish to practice. (Profound!) Matthew 23:13 (KJV) states, "But woe to you, scribes and Pharisees, hypocrites, because you shut off the kingdom of heaven from men; for you do not enter yourselves, nor do you allow those who are entering to go in." Matthew 23:28 (KJV) states, "Even so you too outwardly appear righteous to men, but inwardly you are full of hypocrisy and lawlessness."

One must remember, our Father is not a god of confusion! The human body is His chamber; it was designed to have an enjoyable, lawful love relationship with Him, which in turn is enjoyed with each other. But if we do not understand the fundamentality within, how can we see Christ spiritually? Those who we depend on to help us see this truth are the very ones who are raping our virginity (our innocence). We were given this structure (body) to embody the very essence of our Creator's power, not a body to flaunt as we see fit. Society has implanted in the minds of our children that females needs to be 32-24-36 in measurement to be desirable and males need to have rippling muscles tearing through their shirts and pants, like a hulk. Whose idea was it anyway of what a perfect body should look like? God made the body in perfection for His glory. His glory is to represent His characteristic of love. The curvature of the female body is for the enjoyment of her husband, and his muscular body is the strength of his wife and family. The female body embodies so much more, for she not only feeds a nation (breast) but carries a nation within her. We are living in an electronic age where just about everything is on the Internet.

One can see young women portraying themselves in the nude, as if they are selling themselves on a platter to the highest bidder. Some would call it art and say they are just showing their sexuality, but when does that sexuality go too far? Many are raising young children. Are they thinking of these children and what they may expose them to? What about the job market? Employers are now asking for Facebook information, and what will they find?

We forget that there are guidelines that we live by and govern our lives, and when we zoom past these guidelines, unaware of the circumstances to our behavior, we face unpleasant consequences. How many of our youths notice the stop signs in their daily routine? Life is a rush for many of them until they hit rock bottom. I have passed many of our young, and the music is so loud that it can be heard a whole block away from their vehicles. They are in their zone and are unaware of their surrounding area, as they press the gas pedal to the floor and off they go. The feeling of fearlessness takes over, and nothing else matters at that moment, as they weave in and out of traffic. Life is a thrill. The restraint is gone. I have seen it many times with the bikers on the highways. I have also seen many a teardrops of parents and good friends as a result of these mindless youths, who share a thrill for a moment in time. The God-fearing light that could have enlightened someone has been shut off forever.

At that moment, life seems meaningless. And when we zoom past the guidelines set up for our safety, we face unpleasant consequences.

Additionally, order was put in the body from creation through systems and pathways. Whenever these systems or pathways are compromised, everything goes contrary to God's law, and this creates or sets up a degrading of the whole creative process.

God's Divinity through Systems

God has taken such tenderness in creating man that He put systems in place to keep us alive, most we learn of in school for example.

These specific systems are widely studied in human anatomy. Human systems are also present in many other animals, such as these:

- Circulatory system—pumping and channeling blood to and from the body and lungs with the heart, blood, and blood vessels
- Digestive system—digesting and processing food with salivary glands, esophagus, stomach, liver, gallbladder, pancreas, intestines, rectum, and anus

If we are rushed to the hospital in time, there are some things man is able to repair, but there are just some things that is beyond what man can do to save a person when we break through some of these systems:

- Endocrine system—communication within the body using hormones made by endocrine glands, such as the hypothalamus, pituitary glands, pineal body or pineal gland, thyroid, parathyroids, and adrenals
- Integumentary system—skin, hair, fat, and nails
- Lymphatic system—structures involved in the transfer of lymph between tissues and the blood stream and includes the lymph and the nodes and vessels
- Muscular system—allows for manipulation of the environment, provides locomotion, maintains posture, and produces heat and includes only skeletal muscle, not smooth muscle or cardiac muscle
- Nervous system—collecting, transferring, and processing information with brain, spinal cord, and peripheral nervous system

- Reproductive system—the sex organs, such as ovaries, fallopian tubes, uterus, vagina, mammary glands, testes, vas deferens, seminal vesicles, and prostate
- Respiratory system—the organs used for breathing, such as the pharynx, larynx, trachea, bronchi, lungs, and diaphragm
- Skeletal system—structural support and protection with bones, cartilage, ligaments, and tendons
- Urinary system—kidneys, ureters, bladder, and urethra involved in fluid balance, electrolyte balance, and excretion of urine

Most of the above systems are learned in high school, but what we did not learn is how these systems are impacted through sexual experiences. Many of the young are clueless to these systems and how they came about, and so they struggle to understand the things they do, such as their likes, dislikes, hate, covetousness, troublesomeness, and backbiting. Paul wrote in Romans 7:15, "For that which I do I allow not; for what I would, that do I not but what I hate that I do." There is a connection with these systems from brain to womb.

The Bible speaks clearly of what we behold that changes us. What does that mean to a youth when we leave it there? What makes us crave those things that should be untouchable to us, for example, something/someone that does not belong to us? What connection can be made to the youth using the system? What happens when we invoke a thought, and what happens in the body to say it's a right or a wrong thought? And how do we deal with that thought? Society declares that if you want something bad enough, you will do everything to get it. So where does this desire stop? Youths are killing for a pair of sneakers, a coat, or anything they can covet. What system comes into play when one covets another man's wife, girlfriend, or boyfriend? The digestive, nervous, and all systems become involve.

In terms of listening to music, most of these role models leave nothing to the imagination. I have listened to songs such as "It Wasn't Me." This song degrades our young women, as if they don't have a brain or intellect. One can see lies and deception in this song, but this is what our young male and females rock to, without a thought to the subliminal message being placed in their heads. Through the continuum of the song, the young man said it wasn't him, even though his girlfriend caught him in every position and stage there were of sexual misconduct.(Source of song:www.azlyrics.com)

(Open up, man) What do you want, man?
(My girl just caught me) You let her catch you?
(I don't know how I let this happen) With who?
(The girl next door, you know) Man
(I don't know what to do) Say it wasn't you
(Alright)
Honey came in and she caught me red-handed
Creeping with the girl next door

A lie is perpetrated, and a girl is hurt. But who cares? It's just a song.

The first time I heard this song, I was picking up my daughter and a couple of her friends from college, and they were swaying back and forth to the song. So I paid attention to the words of the song, and I found it offensive. I turned down the music and asked my daughter and her friends if they ever stopped to really listen to the words, and they said no. I repeated some of the lyrics to them and asked them how they felt about what's being said, and they were like, "Oh, Mom, it's only music." And I said, "No, this is not only music. This is how some young man is going to treat you because they think you all are fools." I asked what girl is going to see her boyfriend in all these compromising position and accept his reason that it wasn't him. They stopped dancing. My daughter who is now married and has three small children of her own now pays more attention intensely to what a guy says and does from that conversation. It is sad that musicians have to write lyrics such as these to get their music sold to the youth. It only goes to show the mind-set of our youths. These types of music sodomized the innocence of our youths.

The group Xscape sings "My Little Secret," which is explicitly about cheating. There is no boundary to what the mind craves. Listening to this song, it's about infatuation, lust, and cheating. There is no respect there for the girlfriend in the picture who doesn't know. Watching the video on Youtube, it would intrigue many young minds to try this sensuality. But in reality, which young person would want that to happen to them? It makes keeping such a secret pleasurable to the perverted mind. It's the intrigue that excites, but at the end of the day, what was or might have been pleasurable in the beginning can turn downright deadly. As my mother would say, "One day you have got to pay the piper." As the author Omraam Mikhaël says, "The devil doesn't come with a pick and a fork but through seduction and intrigued."

This is another song, which was done by the artist Enrique Iglesias, "My girlfriend is out of town / And I'm all alone / Your boyfriend is on vacation / And he doesn't have to know / No one can do the things I'm gonna wanna to do to you." These are just to name a few. These are what our youths are listening to, and we wonder where the morality has gone. This is the thought of one of our musicians, and he is so correct about the feeling that lets one loses control of their sense of good judgment, "Well, this might outright be an intimate song, but I do not understand the feeling that I get when I hear this. There's just so much more to the song than pointing out physical intimacy. For me, beyond that, it also speaks of the roller-coaster kind of happiness that you feel when you're with the ones you love. But I still suggest that you do not sing this to a random girl who's not really that comfortable with you yet as you may sound like a maniac."

What this musician is saying here is true to the end of his statement (sounds like a maniac). In the paper last 2012, a young man was sent to jail for killing his girlfriend, and the paper said they had such promising future. And now one future is gone because she is dead, and the other is left to work out a jail sentence. Not that this situation has anything to do with these songs, but this is an example of rage toward his girlfriend who wanted to end the relationship. Another is the incident that recently happened in which a pro football player, Jovan Belcher, killed his girlfriend and also himself due to jealousy. When sex becomes a part of a relationship, as I have said before, when two become spiritually connected and usually if one wants to end the relationship and the other doesn't, pain is created, which sometimes lead to death, as in this case.

Due to the ungodly influences out there, our youth's vocabulary broadens daily. They have incorporated the *next*, which means if this relationship doesn't work, just move on to the next and the next and the next. And in most cases, the next takes them farther and farther from God, as the minds become cold toward the Word of God. Their experience many times makes them become bitter and callous, and it is harder to reach their minds in a godly way. Like I said before, one doesn't see pain but one feels pain. And depending on how intense the pain, one will kill if that individual is not caught in time to (as we say) talk some sense into him or her.

As one piece through the words of Enrique Iglesias, "roller-coaster kind of happiness," what comes to mind? A daze, a churn in the stomach, a sweaty palm, and all the erotic emotions, just as the song sung by Tina Turner, there is a confused & dazzled look on the individual face. What desire is being invoked? Promiscuity? Lies? How would a girl/boy feel away from their friend only to find or hear rumors of them being with someone else? What is he insinuating also that you need to make sure there is a sense of comfort?

I was placed in a situation ten years ago on my job where I was approached by a male coworker to give him a chance to go out with me. And I was shocked at his request, knowing that one he was married, living at home with his wife and children, and two I was married and living at home with a husband. I was so shocked at his request that I had to leave his office to collect my thoughts. I went to another friend who knew us both and told him about it in which he called my coworker up and asked him if he was crazy and what he was thinking. By the time I returned to my office, my phone rang, and it was the coworker apologizing.

These are people who I had worked with for some fifteen years or, better, had written letters on their behalf, laughed, and talked with. They were comfortable in speaking to me about anything and getting an honest answer, but this time, he crossed the line. I asked him why he would do something like this, and he said he did not think. I would take it that way, and he was sorry. Since then, we were casual to each other, but he never approached me that way again.

I have had a similar situation with another male coworker, who was very clear in what he wanted. And this time, I was more prepared and told him that I would go along with his suggestion based on one thing—that he, his wife, and I sat down and talk about this. He asked me if I was crazy and left. Each time he saw me, he would hide behind a door or a column, if it's outdoors. These people knew me personally as coworkers, but they allow themselves to believe they could pass the line of a working relationship to suit their hidden agenda. There is so much danger lurking for the unsuspecting young. If these situations are not dissected, it is not immediately seen or noticed. Our young are not groomed to dissect or see these things coming; they are not knowledgeable enough to realize because the spiritual eyesight is closed.

Additional Suggestive Communication

What God has put in place can be used for good or evil, but do they know that special look or touch can lead down to the wrong path? Do they know the implication of a kiss, a hug, an erotic dance, and the dress code and that all these areas can lead to much more than they bargain for? No, they don't because it feels good. And who cares? Let's go with the flow. In our society today, we are taught that if you want something bad enough, do anything and everything to get it. People demoralize themselves to be on a TV show. There are billboards sending subliminal messages, which young people on a daily basis see, and they are unaware of the impact it is having on their minds. A young girl may start dressing more provocatively going to school and meeting friends to make an impression. And if that's not enough, here comes mister fast-talking, sweet-talking male figure with the lines "if you were a lollipop, I would lick you all over" or "you are so hot, you sizzle to the touch." And one of the greatest is "if you were my queen, I would love you forever."

Many fall prey to this type of communication. Even though there are males who do consider female bodies precious, they have no qualm in abusing it. The group the O'Jays mentioned in one of their songs "Money, Money, Money," and I quote, "A woman will sell her precious body." There goes the acknowledgment that the body is precious indeed, but how does one makes it perfectly clear to our youths how important their bodies are? With so much happening in their lives, how do we expect them to handle those emotions in a sensible and practical way?

As there are systems in the body, so as there are systems in heaven being held together by one source—the Universal Creator. How can our young understand God's love if they don't understand their own bodies in a spiritual way—the chemistry that runs through our veins, which makes us who we are in the creative process? I remember as a young teen, my mom used to say, "A woman who learns how to control her body, controls her life." But that's all that was said, and the quote stops there. It's a taboo of speaking of sexual things, so as teens, we go on in darkness, learning by mistakes after mistakes after mistakes until the bulb goes off to some of us. And sometimes by the time we get that revelation, we have already done so much to ourselves and to others. I have had the opportunity of speaking to many young adults and was told that the lessons they learn were so brutal that they had wished to know some of the things I talked about in this book. One of these young adults I spoke with was my dear and beautiful, little friend Tiffany. I met Tiffany while working in a girls' group home. Tiffany was one of those teens given to the government. In interviewing this young lady on how she became sexually active and the things that could or should have been done to persuade her otherwise to think about her action, these are some of her words, "I wished that I was told how precious my body was by my parents, but they were too busy arguing and fighting. I had no idea of the many diseases that was out there that I could have gotten. I was only thirteen years old when I started having sex for the first time with a boy from my school. I was in love with him [or so she thought]." I asked her how she knew she was in love, and she said, "Well, after sex, I felt so connected to him." What she did not understand was she had bonded herself to him spiritually. It's not something one sees, but it's an emotion one feels. This is the reason when one or the other goes contrary to what the other believes as together forever, it brings devastation to many and bitterness, for we fornicate in the mind first before we bear the brunt of our action(s).

When I met Tiffany, she had marks all over her arms, as if someone had meticulously sliced into them. Eventually, in talking to her, I found out that she would cut herself because each cut represent pain to the young man she had become connected to. To some, this frame of mind makes no sense as one would think she was only hurting herself. But in her mind, she is not hurting herself but another. This is where many of our youths are in their thinking, "connected to him." Amy Fisher, a sixteen-year-old, also felt this connection when she started having sex with the married Joey Buttafuoco in 1991 to the point of trying to kill his wife to gain him for herself. A song came to mind as she said she felt so connected to him, which Madonna sang, "Like a Virgin." How many young girls feel this way after having sex for the very first time (in this case, willingly) and say they feel connected? If one was to ask them to explain why they feel connected, it would be hard because it is a spiritual thing. As Madonna sang, she was beat, incomplete, sad, and blue. But he made her feel shiny and new to the point that she wants to give all her love (not some but all her love). He made her fear fade so quickly that she felt more bold to the point that she would be his till the end of time. He makes her feel there is nothing to hide, for there is no shame.

I thought to myself as I continued my interview, *Can one feel the deep emotional feeling this young woman is experiencing at this time? Is sex the culprit here, or is it something else?* Many of us can still remember our first encounter in this arena. This is God's domain, which should never be shared with anyone without ample preparation of the heart and mind. I am not saying it is an easy task; I'm saying it is doable. Many are doing it, but unfortunately, it is usually after many painful heartbreaks that the lesson is learned. I asked her if she hadn't had sex, would she feel so connected, and she said, "No, I wouldn't." I asked her if she was in a church at the time all this was happening, would she seek someone to confide in, and she said yes, if she could have found someone to confide in. There is dullness in the minds of many parents to guide their children properly. In Tiffany's case, her home was in turmoil. It was like a battleground because of her parents that they put her in the middle at times to take sides. She felt that she heard things that she should not have known. Her parents put their problems in front of the well-being of their children. Many youth in these situations have found solace in sex and sometimes end up with an unintended pregnancy or something worse. Tiffany has no children and is now twenty-two years old and working. She is a very talented young woman in many ways and a great poet. For most young ladies who have gotten pregnant, I have heard of such talks as "you are not the first, and you certainly are not going to be the last," and this is supposed to be a comfort to some of those teens who goes on to have more babies without the slightest inclination of how much this will impact their future.

One of my dearest friends is a grandmother of eight grandchildren. Out of these eight children, one parent has five children. Each child was conceived while the young lady was still living at home with her parents. In as much as this young lady knew that the father of her children was living with someone else, it did not matter. The young man went on to impregnate several other young ladies, the youngest child being under a year. The last female knew of his other children and even knew that he was not supporting his other children and still went on to become pregnant. After the child was born, several months later, she realized that she was not getting the support from him either and took him to court for support. Now one has to wonder what went wrong with these pictures. The morality and self-esteem are completely broken. Now there are those whom our youths idolize (and I may touch a nerve to many), but let the truth be told. Not that these are bad people because they more than likely came up with the same system of not knowing, but they shine in the eyes of our youth, such as Jay Z, Beyonce, Nikki Minaj, Madonna, Justin, Rihanna, and so many others. These are the news flash that shows up on the tabloids, drawing our youths to want to know who is sleeping with who, who is being attacked but wants to have a baby with such a person, who is married to someone else but is pregnant for another, who is pregnant for an old crush before while that crush is still married to his wife, or who is fighting with who to get attention. This is what intrigues our youths. These are the kinds of sensations that draw and appeal to us to want to know. If there is already a problem with young female pregnancy, what are they getting from these messages being sent through the tabloids, Youtube, and elsewhere? And unfortunately, some of their favorite idols do nothing more than accelerate the problem. Alicia Keys, who is so well loved, was apparently dating her husband before he's divorced and became pregnant before her marriage to him. Now Kim Kardashian, who is still married to Kris Humphries, is now pregnant for Kanye West and now is his baby mama, as he so joyfully blurted out at one of his concerts. I remember when the words *baby mama* send a negative charge, but now is it going to be even more accepting in taste?

These ignites the imagination of our youths of today with their music and movies, but all have a story line that our youth do not know because they are caught up in the euphoria of lust, which dulls the senses of what to be wary of. These actions to our youths are acceptable norms. Beyonce last year had done a spotlight (stage performance) for the Super Bowl, and it was well received (applauded) by the crowd (audience). It was seductive, enchanting, intriguing, enticing, and loud. What comes through for most of these shows is that sex sells. In my youth, it was the soap opera, The *Young and the Restless*, *General Hospital*, and *All My Children*. I will never forget the summer when Luke and Lara left town and was on the run. The TV rooms at the colleges were packed. From those soaps, I learned how to cheat, not trust, and how to fall senselessly in love with a fool, disregarding the consequences to follow. It finally dawned on me one day, as I pushed my way through the crowd of students in the TV room to find out what happen to Luke and Lara, that this is too much, for every time that a couple seems to be happily married, there is going to be infidelity from one or the other spouse somewhere along the line. I turned to a friend one day and said, "I would like to see someone stay together until old age in one of these plots." It was either make up to break up after sex or infidelity in secret. I was done. Just as it played out in these soaps, it is exactly what I saw playing out in my life later but also in friends and acquaintances, yet still many of us were in (so-called) godly homes and attending church week after week.

One evening while riding the bus home, I overheard a conversation between a young woman and her friend (I can only assume it was a female because of the content of the conversation, as she was very loud to the point a few older ladies was not too happy with her words). As she continued the conversation, she was telling her friend that it was her fault for getting pregnant. She went on to say to her friend that if she is going to f——, then at least get something in return. It was hard on the ear, but this young lady did not care because she was angry at her friend. Should I be angry with this young lady for her lack of respect for the surrounding she was in?

Working at a university has given me access to an enormous amount of students from many countries. On several occasions, I have held female students in my arms who were devastated and in tears because of a bad grade, roommate troubles, money issues, or boyfriend issues or who were just plain depressed because of family problems at home. Some I found weeping away in bathrooms or in hallways. One young lady was devastated to the point where it was difficult to calm her down as she threw herself to the floor, crying, because her parents had given away her precious pet while she is studying in the US. Another cried because she found herself pregnant when she was in her last year of school, who was from a single family and was on a scholarship. There was also a young father who had to leave school because of bad grades, who was from a single family (mother and an only child), leaving behind not only school but a brand-new baby girl that he missed dearly. But I am here to say that in each of these events, after speaking with them of the love of Christ and opening up the importance of who they are in a spiritual way, these people left my presence with a different perspective than before when we met. Other students of whom I am not familiar were not as fortunate as they ended their lives in suicide. I am not here to speak on our counseling intervention of our youth but I am here to state emphatically that if there is no spiritual intervention when counseling our youths, we have already lost the battle. The parent of one of the suicide victims said in an interview, "Too often universities hide behind these adults who are employed there when it comes to making decisions about a student's well-being. Nobody should be losing people to suicide—certainly not young people, certainly not the brightest minds there are." I say yes, these are bright minds, but what spiritual foundation do they have before leaving home? What strong spiritual anchor do they have when things get rough out there?

The Physical vs. the Spiritual

We are physical and spiritual people all intertwined, but if we do not understand how to ascertain the difference, we are bound to have tragedies in our lives. I am sure when Adam saw Eve in the garden for the first time, it was not a woman flesh of my flesh but a woman flesh or my flesh, no different than in our time, when a man sees a woman and says wow, whether it's for her shapely beauty or facial beauty. The problem is, how far does that attraction go and how do we keep it in check? We find beauty in so many physical ways—face, feet, hands, fingers, nails, you name it because that's all is seen but not the harmonizing of God's handiwork. Paul gives us an example of the uniqueness of the body as being physical and spiritual. It is all we have need of and how it all comes together in harmony to become peace.

We find peace in different ways. Some through yoga, vigorous exercise, reading a book, going to a spa, walking, mountain climbing, meditating, praying, spending time with a loved one, counseling, having a day out with friends, and sometimes being alone watching the sunset. I am sure there are other ways that is not mentioned here, but at some point, that yearning for peace comes alive in each of us. We need quiet time with the Father. At times I go to work a little earlier than usual to spend time in his Word or on Saturdays in the back of my home, sitting outside under a tree. There was a time when I gravitate to everyone that I thought could explain deeply the things of God, but in my journey, I was badly hurt by those I trusted to that end until the day I spoke openly to God and said, "If you want me to know you, well, you better start teaching because I am done." And I believe that's when my true journey started. Our youths do not know about quiet time with the master of the universe. Quiet time for our youth is when they are asleep. As soon as their eyes are open, it is go, go, go. Where do they learn this? Grown adults and television. Many are beaten and tired by the time they make it through college, if they even finish.

Please read 1 Corinthians 12:12–26. The body was made uniquely to be a useful tool for enjoyment, to nourish, to praise, and to love. It was created to harmonize everything in its space. Even though Paul stayed away from the sexual organs, he showed the harmony/attachment of each to one another. Looking at the female's and male's body, one sees a perfect imagery as God planned—her breast to not only feed a nation through the milk it gives containing the necessary immunity to strengthen the new infant while nurturing it at the same time. Breast milk is not only the best way to feed your newborn or infant, but this nourishing substance has the ability to heal and protect the body as well. According to the *Webster's New World Medical Dictionary*, *breast milk* is "milk from the breast." Human milk contains a balance of nutrients that closely matches infant requirements for brain development, growth, and healthy immune system. Human milk also contains immunologic agents and other compounds that act against viruses, bacteria, and parasites. Since an infant's immune system is not fully developed until age two, human milk provides a distinct advantage.

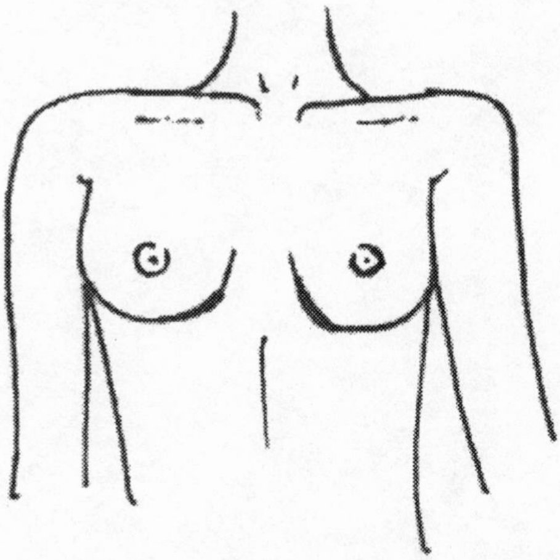

Breastfeeding

The vagina, which gives hope to the creation of a new being and which sheds blood, cleansing the female's body, should be protected at all cost. But instead, it is used as a welcome doormat to every Tom, Dick, and Harry that comes by looking for a warm body. The opening was not placed there for mere enjoyment and entertainment. This goes well for the male who has a tube called the penis extended from his body by which semen is ejaculated into the vagina to complete a work, creating a masterpiece most pleasing to God.

When a young girl looks into the mirror, she should be seeing God's handiwork, a platform for life, something to be cherished, not to give away needlessly. This body has a purpose. It is God's looking glass through each generation. So is the same for a young man. What does he see when he looks at himself in the mirror? Does he see God's inspired image or a body of bulky muscles rippling through and through? I can tell you what he sees. It's a self-centered image of one who is going to conquer the world and dazzle the girls.

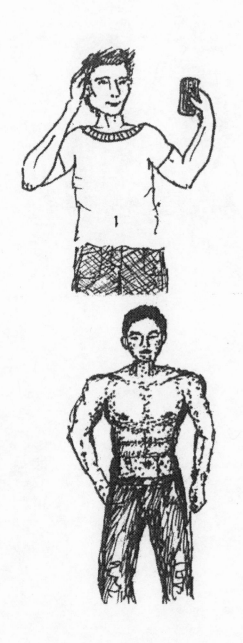

What a girl sees is how lean or fat she is or what image she wants to portray to a guy.

Little do they know that they are being set up to enter and battle a system of bigotry and lies, where some will make it through to old age and some will not.

We are powerful beyond measure, but if we do not understand that power, we are doomed to continue repeating error after error.

Our youths would not be familiar with this movie because it would be long before their time, but for those of us who might remember, what did Thulsa Doom know in the film of *Conan the Barbarian* (1982)? "There was a time, boy, when I searched for steel, when steel meant more to me than gold or jewels. Steel isn't strong, boy, flesh is stronger!" Steel is quite strong, but what is it compared to the will of mankind? What message is being referenced here? It's not about the flesh but about the mind of an individual. He realized that if one can control the mind, then the flesh will follow without any problem. It is through the gateway of the mind that one needs to stimulate for everything to follow. There is a group of people who is hell-bent on doing just that, and we call them radicals. Their minds are completely saturated and focused on doing whatever is necessary to complete one task, and that is to change the world under their ideology even if it means dying in the process. We fear these individuals, but there is no fear to our children to die without knowing God. Yet still we cry out to the Creator when devastation hits our cities. Doesn't it sound familiar from days of old? Who is to be blamed? The government, the churches, or our pride? We have youths changing hands and crossing borders for what they believe of doing something good for their belief of the good. Their minds have been infiltrated by hatred and darkness, so we now have these cells (as it's called) within our society. So tell me, who is safe?

Sex Slavery

When one think of sex slavery, we immediately think of women or men who are sexually abused in other countries and also in the United States. But it never comes to mind the ravaging of our youths' minds when it comes to the movies they watch, the songs they hear, the clothes they wear, or the line of cosmetics they are open to. The mind is the strongest asset to any human being, and depending on what happens to that individual from the day they are conceived in the womb till the day they die is what makes the difference.

As a nation, we failed miserably in protecting our youths for in them locked up the jewels of heaven. If proper preparation was introduced early at appropriate ages, then there would be a generation more apt to maintain a more moral upright and spiritual (godly nature) nation/generation. So as sex was at the helm, so will it be at the end. Sexual taboos lead to an infestation of disgust, a downhill spiraling of the human nations. This is an out-of-control generation where sex becomes perverted. This was never the intention of the Creator.

Beauty of Sex

Sex was meant for a more mature frame of mind. From research, it was shown the side of beauty that completes sex. Let's look at some of its benefits:

- Relieves stress
- Lowers blood pressure
- Boosts immunity
- Counts as exercise
- Improves cardiovascular health
- Boosts self-esteem
- Strengthens one's well-being
- Improves intimacy
- Reduces pain
- May reduce prostate cancer risk (*British Journal of Urology International*)
- Strengthens pelvic floor muscle
- Improves sleep

Does this seem like something the Creator would have wanted to hold back from us? No, but He who creates us knows full well the damage that can come from this action without the proper preparation. All this speaks one thing—harmony. He who has made us has set in motion certain hormones in the body to facilitate the sexual act of enjoyment. It's interesting that it starts in the brain. For example, oxytocin, referred to as the sex hormone, is best known for its role in sexual reproduction. Studies have been done showing the activities of this hormone in a pleasurable condition. What is interesting is that oxytocin decreases in negative circumstances, such as bad relationship. Oxytocin is a polypeptide hormone produced by the posterior lobe of the pituitary gland that stimulates contraction of the smooth muscle of the uterus.

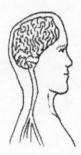

(This is a direct relationship of the brain and uterus.) Think about where you would physically feel a gut feeling.

Research has shown that the network of neurons lining our guts is so extensive that it has now been nicknamed our second brain or other brain. This gut "brain" doesn't think for us, but it does play a key role in certain diseases and communicates with the brain in our skull. Our "second brain" is known as the enteric nervous system (Medicinenet.com). Is it possible to show them the connection of when they make decision(s) and how it affects the nervous system? Why do they have the ache in their stomach when they have a headache? And how does this wonderful hormone decrease when the body is going through crisis? I remember my first heartbreak while I was still in high school. My boyfriend, who later became my husband, broke up with me, and the pain I felt in my stomach was unbearable. I had no concept what was going on except but that it hurt and caused my body grief. Is it possible that if there was no sexual act between us that the hurt would not be as bad? Why is it when people go through tragedies—whether it's a death, bad news, or lovesickness—the pain is so harsh that they hold their bellies? The eternal and everlasting God thought of this before we knew of it, and so He placed hormones in our bodies to help in these situations, for everyone goes through extreme situations at one time or another. No one is immune to this. It is said that oxytocin plays some crucial roles in our bodies in helping us to stave off a number of psychological and physiological problems. Oxytocin gives us the ability to break down barriers when meeting new people, and it helps us to build positive self-esteem. And because the hormone plays such an important role in trust and building relationships, wounds can be healed, damaged relationships can sometimes be fixed, and trauma can be overcome. It is said that every cell in the body has a tightly regulated system that dictates when it needs to grow, mature, and eventually die off.

When one thinks of these things, how can one not believe in a supreme god, a divine hand in our lives? Do our youths need to be medical students to understand this creative process of an eternal God? I don't think so.

The simple act of bodily contact will cause your brain to release low levels of oxytocin—both in yourself and in the person you're touching. Often referred to as the "love molecule," oxytocin is typically associated with helping couples establish a greater sense of intimacy and attachment. This explains some of that dazed, confused, roller-coaster kind of happiness, kind of feeling one may experience previously talked about.

Sex Sells, Sex Legalized, Sex Enslaves

I remember when one had to be at an appropriate age to view sexual (R-rated) movies or enter certain clubs or bars. Now Hollywood opens up the gate to inquisitive minds, sex sells. They call it entertainment, and it began a legalizing that seems to have no end. These attractions completely dull the righteous senses. We need not go too far from home because it is all there for our "enjoyment," not only from the old but also the young. There is none or almost no constraint on passion after visualizing these acts, especially if there is alcohol involved. In these situations, boundaries can be overridden if one does not understand the sweeping effects of this emotion. In the Bible, Herod, the Edomite king, committed murder while under the influence of alcohol and was being seduced by a seductive dance of the daughter of Herodias. His regret later on could not be revered as the death of John the Baptist was done. His sexual desire was of such that he completely lost sight of practicality and called the death of one of Christ's greatest servant, John the Baptist.

Jesus said in the Sermon on the Mount that it is not only wrong to commit adultery, it is wrong to think adultery (Matt. 5:27–28). The following words came from the very mouth of Christ, "But the fearful, and unbelieving, and the abominable, and murderers, and whoremongers, and sorcerers, and idolaters, and all liars, shall have their part in the lake that burns with fire and brimstone" (Rev. 21:8). The word *whoremonger* is from the Greek word usually rendered as "fornicator." Our youths just need a firm but loving hand to pull them up and to give them something to hold firmly onto without any wavering.

Crisis of Sex through Role Modeling

It is not enough to say to young adults to abstain and not have sex because the Bible says so; they want sound explanation that makes sense to them because this is what we are up against at this time. Many celebrities are having babies and are not married, and some are contemplating having babies and are still not married. For example, Rihanna is asking for time off from her business just to become pregnant for Chris Brown even though she knows that he has a newborn with someone else recently and was actually living with that person. Chris Brown was also accused of beating and battering Rihanna only a year ago, and this was all over the tabloids. Now what message is being sent to our youths who look up to these individuals as role models? What about the sitcom *Sex and the City* and *Friends*, which portray sexual acts with different male partners? These are some of the criticisms made relating to the show: Criticism has been expressed about the influence the show has on adolescents and how the images displayed on the show affect the way women and young girls view themselves. *Sex and the City*, along with the sitcom *Friends*, were specifically recognized for "glamori[zing] sex while hardly mentioning its downsides, such as pregnancy and sexually transmitted diseases" by a 2008 study published in the *American Journal of Pediatrics*. The study found that females twelve to seventeen who watched these and similarly "sexually charged" shows were about twice as likely to get pregnant as those who did not, and teenage male viewers were more likely to impregnate someone. The Daily Mail article noted that similar studies have also found an association between viewing sexual content and earlier sex and higher disease risk. All this is to say, depending on the age, give them the raw facts. And one of the raw facts is this: as former US surgeon Gen. C. Everett Koop has said, "When you have sex with someone, you are having sex with everyone they have had sex with for the last ten years and everyone they and their partners have had sex within the last ten years."

Today is not the time to be closed-minded when speaking to our teen (depending on maturity). Ask them how they feel about this kind of exposure.

You will hear phrases such as gross, nasty, or wow because this would be the farthest thing from their minds. Teens many times live in denial and think things won't happen to them because they may use contraceptive means (condom, for example), but if it bursts, what then? Some may say their friend would not lie to them about using contraceptives, but ask them, are they willing to take the chance? Most times guys are relying on girls to use protection, and many pregnancies come about because of this. I have seen plenty of hurt in this way, and the pain is deep. As I have said before, I have worked in several group homes and have seen firsthand as to what length boys and girls will go to have sex. I have seen parents who have kept anger in for years because they have given themselves to another without thinking of the consequences of their action. And when their expectation is not met (in many cases, marriage), they carry anger for most, if not, the rest of their and their child or children from those relationships suffer. Children from these kind of traumatic relationships many times continue this same trauma into their adult life (this is what most of us call baggage). This ripple effect will trickle down to generations if it is not stopped by someone outside of the family or a family member, who is familiar with psychological traumas, to bring the awareness to the family.

Issue to the Attention of Someone

These are the people who sometimes grow up to hate God, as they believe God was not there for them when they were being abused. These are the ones who need Him more than anything in their lives. These are the ones who need much empathy but sometimes feel they have no problem and need no one's empathy or sympathy. Many of these are the ones coming out of lockup or foster homes for most of their lives. Many of these youths are individuals who are without mothers or fathers to care for them and have become the responsibility of the government.

I have seen guys who will not take responsibility for their actions because they believe they were tricked, duped, or whatever. A week ago an officer was sentenced for killing his eighteen-year-old girlfriend by shooting her in the head and driving her car to an apartment complex, leaving his eleven-month-old daughter strapped in her seat and left abandoned in the car for days. By the time the child was found, she was dead. He did this to keep him from being taken to court to pay child support because he denied the child as his. He was forty years old; she was a youth.

Out of Harmony

When we are out of harmony in the body, this creates stress as shown in early pregnancy, partnership breakup, argument, guilt, anger, frustration, denial, and death. Let's look at how stress can throw the body in an unbalanced state. Did you know that the emotional and physical responses you have to stress are set in motion by a series of chemical releases and reactions? Find out what is really going on inside your body.

The Emotional Brain—Limbic System

The primary area of the brain that deals with stress is its limbic system. Because of its enormous influence on emotions and memory, the limbic system is often referred to as the emotional brain.

Distress Signals from Your Brain

The adrenal glands release adrenaline (also known as epinephrine) and other hormones that increase breathing, heart rate, and blood pressure. This moves more oxygen-rich blood faster to the brain and to the muscles needed for fighting or fleeing. And you have plenty of energy to do either because adrenaline causes a rapid release of glucose and fatty acids into your bloodstream. Other hormones shut down functions unnecessary during the emergency. Growth, reproduction, and the immune system all go on hold. Blood flow to the skin is reduced. That's why chronic stress leads to sexual dysfunction, increases your chances of getting sick, and often manifests as skin ailments.

Stress Compromises the Blood-Brain Barrier

Stress can dramatically increase the ability of chemicals to pass through the blood-brain barrier.

As science gains greater insight into the consequences of stress on the brain, the picture that emerges is not a pretty one. A chronic overreaction to stress overloads the brain with powerful hormones that are intended only for short-term duty in emergency situations. Their cumulative effect damages and kills brain cells. Yi years ago, one of my daughters lost a friend, who ended her life by shooting herself in the head, leaving her two-year-old son. This was overwhelming stress brought on by an abundance of responsibility caring for her son. There was little to no cooperation from her son's father, and she already was having a strained relationship with her mother. One day the crisis was too much for her as she called her son's father, telling him to tell her son she loved him, and he could hear the shot over the phone.

In 2004 I had to speak to a young man in long distance who was from a single mom and an only child, who had fathered a child while in college. I worked with a young lady who worked in the office with me. They were both in college at the time. They both started having problems after the child was born in juggling school and for her work and for him keeping up with school work and being a part of the athletic team. The young lady was given a full scholarship in her last year of college, and he also had a scholarship. They started arguing about who would keep the child until he pulled away and started dating someone else. She was devastated. In making a long story short, we kept the baby in the office at times until she was able to get a sitter. In the meantime, the young man lost his scholarship and was sent back to his home state. She told me about it in which I called the young man several times until he answered the phone. He explained that he wanted to die because he felt he had failed his mother, girlfriend, child, and himself. We spoke each day on my lunch hour, and we prayed. He and the young lady started communicating again. He got into a church, and the last time we spoke, he was doing well. It took a little while, but he came to recognize and understand the recklessness of living outside of God's plan for his life, and he made some changes. He accepted his errors and had a renewed spirit and wanted to help others in not making the same mistakes that he made. The young lady continued in college and was able to graduate. She is now married with three additional children and a husband.

The Bible teaches peace, continual peace. Human beings were created to dominate this planet and live in a peaceful environment with one another, as well as the animal and insect kingdom.

Stress is no respecter of anyone, young or old. And where there is no harmony, there is disharmony, and disharmony within can create disease.

Parents should seek to interest their children in the study of physiology. There are but a few among the youths who have definite knowledge of the mysteries of life. Although God says to them, "Beloved, I wish above all things that thou mayest prosper and be in health, even as thy soul prosper," yet they do not understand the influence of the body upon the mind or of the mind upon the body (*Testimonies for the Church* vol. 7, 65). The study of the wonderful human organism, the relation and dependence of its complicated parts, is one in which many parents take little interest. Neither is it taught in the churches.

Many of our youths have lost their lives because chronic stress has entered their lives, and they do not know where to turn, or they are too ashamed to turn to anyone.

Excess physical, chemical, or emotional pressure causes a stress reaction in the body. The stress reaction is a state of "overdrive" where our organs work overtime to enable us to keep functioning when under pressure—our fight-or-flight response. Take a look at the chain reaction that occurs in the body when we are stressed and the areas of the body that is affected.

These are the areas of the body affected by stress:

- Muscles and joints
- Heart
- Stomach
- Pancreas
- Intestines
- Reproductive system
- Brain
- Adrenaline glands
- Nervous system
- Liver
- Blood pressure
- Pancreas

Sex is a gift from God to fill the earth to have people whom He can dwell among and people whose thought would be as his thought and people who would be able to behold him face-to-face without any veil of partition between him and them one day. This creator we have come to know by so many names has always wanted to be among his people. Exodus 25:8 states, "Let them make me a sanctuary that I may dwell among them." The sanctuary went everywhere the people went. The sanctuary was very important to Him, and it still is. Each child that is born of the womb (his sanctuary) should be sanctified by truth before they are introduced to this world. Research has shown that babies welcome the voice of their parents long before they are born. John 17:17 states, "Sanctify them through thy truth thy word is truth." So it is the continued word of truth that our youths need and preferably starting at an early age.

Come Let Us Reason

He wants reasoning individuals to make well-thought-out decisions. If this was not so, He would not have said in Isaiah 1:18, "Come now, let us reason together." In today's life, we are all too busy to find time to reason with our youths, and those who may find a little time don't know where to either start or are too scared to even approach the subject. How many of us have really looked at our little ones and said it's time for some rational talk?

Not too many, because by the time we even have the thought of speaking to our youth, they already have learned a lot from peers, media, and elsewhere (they are doing the job for us), so their minds are closed to us before we even start. Some of our youths are asking, "Why now?" They feel at this point, they know what they need to know, so they are not willing to listen to most things, if not anything parents or those in authority have to say. Those youths may have gone through or are going through changes at one time or another and needed help, but family pressures may not have been ideal for parent(s) to notice the need, so it goes unattended for a time. For that youth, the question is "Why now?" when parents are ready to talk. Their attitude is more of "now that you have time for me, I don't have time for you."

How many times parents may hear, "Mom/Dad, you don't understand!"? At this time for parents and child, it's like being on two different planets speaking two different languages. Reasoning is hard work; we can see this from the Word of God. If it wasn't so, we wouldn't be seeing the term stiff-necked people. "Jerusalem, Jerusalem thou that killeth the prophets and stone them which are sent unto thee, how often would I have gathered thy children together, even as a hen gathereth her chickens under her wing and you would not" (Matt. 23:37). God has been pleading with his people for a very long time. Reasoning takes time and great effort. If we are to reach our youth with reasoning, it is going to take much time, effort, and prayers. As parents, we are not only battling the economic climate but the technological era in which we live. For many, technology has taken hold of our children before they are even able to speak, and we call it building intelligence. We use the television/media to pacify our young children to keep them quiet as we leave them in front of the television to absorb and keep their attention, as lesser and lesser time is spent from the human hands for nourishment and nurturing. Our youths are hungry for knowledge, but their anger and frustration keep them in bondage due to the wear and tear of everyday life. If this was not so, celebrities would not be making so much money with music, following them on Twitter, Facebook, blogs, Instagram and doing the new one out there, selfie. I wonder what is going to come next? It says in 2 Timothy 3, "This know also, that in the last days perilous times shall come, for men will be lovers of themselves, covetous, boasters, proud, blasphemers, disobedient to parents, unthankful, unholy." Does that sound like what's going on now?

These youths are searching for a place to be comfortable to meet, greet, and express themselves in terms they can understand. What we have is a spiritually starved generation of youths.

As I have said before, I have had the privilege of working with many youths, and I have found them to be open-minded (by that I mean to anything good or bad), happy-go-lucky people. In one of these group homes that I worked in, there was a young man who showed many good qualities. I found him to be kind and gentle, respectful to all the adults who worked there. However this young man decided in his mind one night to steal my keys to my vehicle and go joyriding. The next morning, this young man also alerted me to the fact that my vehicle was badly damaged when he went outside to play ball. After calling the police, he was interviewed by them. As they pressed him for the truth, the result was that he took my keys unknown to me and left the house very late that night and went driving and lost control of the vehicle, damaging it badly. The following days after, he presented me with the following letter.

I have also had the privilege of accompanying several college-age students from George Washington University and Maryland University, who came together under the umbrella of a fine gentleman and chaplain to harness the hope and passion in many shut-in youths in the Washington, DC, area, that there is hope for them to be viable citizens in society and help others and to attend a higher education. I have attended panel talks in which police officers spoke of youths that they have picked up from the streets and have asked parents to come to the precinct to pick up their children, and there was no response. Mothers have been known to drop their children off and said they will return and never do. This is what we see happening in our society every day. Circumstances have worn so many mothers to the ground that they themselves have lost hope. Many of these homes are without mature male figures who are willing to sacrifice and live godly lives, and so the youths of that home is left to their own demise.

In Isaiah 49:15, the Lord says, "Can a mother forget a child who nurses at her breast and have compassion on the son of her womb?"

Our youths are lacking true friendships, and so they find them anywhere they can get them. How many times have we truly cuddled our youths? And I am not speaking of spoiling them with any and everything they want but with a love of showing them you are there for them. One morning heading to work on the bus, I witnessed a mother who came on the bus only with the intention of clearing up a situation that happened a day before on the bus. Apparently, what was said was that her son was misbehaving on the bus and cursed at a woman. Even though his grandmother was on the same bus, she stated that she did not hear her grandson curse. The mother was livid as she explained that she is trying to raise her son right, and if he had done something improperly, she would be the first to have him apologize and deal with him later at home. I got the sense that this is a no-nonsense mother, and she wants to do right in the situation. She did have her son apologize to the woman, but I could see that he did not want to and was very angry as he was trying to defend himself that he did not use the curse words.

After the mother got off the bus, no one spoke to the young man, but he continued to curse under his breath. I left my seat and went over to sit and hug this little boy who sat in front of his grandma. I told him how important he was to his mom and grandma and how much he is loved. I told him that his mom did not come on the bus to embarrass or bawl him out, but because of her love and fairness, she wanted her son to be respectful even when he does not feel like it. I explained that I know it is not easy for him to say "I'm sorry," but it is something we all do when it's needed. I showed him his hand and his feet, how God made him perfect and how wonderful he was made. I told him one day he will have to take care of his mom, and she is expecting to have a strong, healthy, and wonderful man in the future. There will be many mistakes he will make, but these are to teach him lessons of life. As I spoke to him, I could feel the tension in his body lessen; he even laughed at some of my jokes. I told his grandmother, "Hug your grandson. Let him know you are there for him as you assist your daughter in raising him. If his mom does not read to him at nights because she is away, then you read to him." She thanked me as she exited the bus, and I could see she was truly grateful for what I had said. I saw a light on her face that touched my heart.

Love them; they need it so much.

We live in a world that establishes disconnection. We have a lack of community love, and our children are spiritually dying because of it. I told this experience to a friend, and I was told that I should not have hugged that child because people are too eager to sue for child abuse. This is a sad affair when genuine love cannot be shared. We are disconnected as family from the things that we believed that sustained us in the past.

Youth Accountability

In *Psychology Today* (magazine), July 12, 2009, Carl E. Pickhardt, PhD, quotes in "Teaching Your Adolescent Independence," "From what I have seen, there are at least four components to this training: responsibility, accountability, work, and self-help. And this instruction can start as soon as adolescence begins (usually between ages 9 and 13), if not before. Young people who learn independence can often say 'I earned my freedom by acting responsibly' (I did what was right even when it was hard to do), 'I was held accountable for my bad choices and paid for my mistakes' (I faced my consequences), 'I worked to get a lot of what I wanted' (it wasn't all handed to me), 'I developed the resourcefulness to help myself to help deal with difficulty' (I met my problems head-on)."

Young people who seem to get stuck in their dependent ways often have parents who, with the most loving motivation, undermine the growth of independence. So it is obvious if young adults can be aware of all this, then why is it that they cannot be trained to understand sexual things righteously? As older adults, many have become despondent and have left the needed effort, which should be put forth at home. The burden is now left on the government to safeguard our children, and so what we have are safe sex, meaning contraceptives and abortion clinics. A report done by the Guttmacher Institute (February 2012), using data of the national level trend, shows a decline in pregnancies to the lowest ever due to the increased contraceptive use and abortion. In sum, teens appear to be making the decision to be more effective contraceptive users, and their actions are paying off in lower pregnancy, birth, and abortion rates. As I have said before, young adults can make intelligent decisions given the right tools to work with, but is it good enough to make the decision not to have children at an early age based only on using the best contraceptives on the market or realizing the will of God when contemplating having sex? Some may say, "Shouldn't spiritual things be left to the churches?" But I say, "Shouldn't spiritual things begin at home with the church as an anchor? Because if I have read correctly, it is us who are the temple coming together to make up the church."

Many young adults are engaging in anal and oral sex with the thinking that they are saving their virginity for marriage. What makes this any different? They are just as prone to STDs as their counterparts who engage in regular sex. Ceci Connolly, *Washington Post* staff writer, Saturday, March 19, 2005, writes, "Teenagers who takes virginity pledges as a public declarations to abstain from sex are almost as likely to be infected with a sexually transmitted disease as those who never made the pledge. Although young people who sign a virginity pledge delay the initiation of sexual activity, marry at younger ages and have fewer sexual partners, they are also less likely to use condoms and more likely to experiment with oral and anal sex, said the researchers from Yale and Columbia universities." "The sad story is that kids who are trying to preserve their technical virginity are, in some cases, engaging in much riskier behavior," said lead author Peter S. Bearman, a professor at Columbia's Institute for Social and Economic Research and Policy. "From a public health point of view, an abstinence movement that encourages no vaginal sex may inadvertently encourage other forms of alterative sex that are at higher risk of STDs."

I found this particularly interesting: Virginity pledges emerged in the early 1990s based on the theory that young people would remain chaste if they had stronger community support or pressure to remain abstinent. Deborah Roffman, an educator and author of *Sex and Sensibility: The Thinking Parent's Guide to Talking Sense about Sex* said that youths who take virginity pledges are often undereducated about sexual health. I would say something is definitely lost here in the thinking of these young adults. They want to do the right thing by keeping themselves virtuous for the right mate. This is the group that needs educating in the Word of God, for there is clearly some confusion there.

It is clear by the remark made by James Wagoner, president of Advocates for Youth in 2001. He said that that the figures are staggering for those who contracted HIV, became pregnant, or contracted other sexually transmitted diseases.

It is now 2017, and our young people are still struggling with this issue. Chlamydia, according to the Centers for Disease Control, is still the most common of the STD. Their bodies are used like wrecking balls, waiting to be laid to rest in the grave. Many of these same young people are sitting in our churches. Do we sound the alarm on these things? No, we preach sweet-sounding words to the ears while our young die daily for the lack of knowledge for the true Word of God.

Viewpoint of the Lutheran Church as It Relates to Human Sexuality

Human Sexuality: Gift and Trust

For action by the ELCA Churchwide Assembly, August 2009

Sexual love—the complex interplay of longing, erotic attraction, self-giving, and receiving, defined by trust—is a wondrous gift. The longing for connection, however, also can render human beings susceptible to pain, isolation, and harm. The desire for sexual love, therefore, does not by itself constitute a moral justification for sexual behavior. Giving and receiving love always involves mixed motives and limited understanding of individual and communal consequences.

The sharing of love and sexual intimacy within the mutuality of a mature and trusting relationship can be a rich source of romance, delight, creativity, imagination, restraint, desire, pleasure, safety, and deep contentment that provides the context for individuals, family, and the community to thrive.

Though sexual love remains God's good gift, sin permeates human sexuality, as it does all of life. When expressed immaturely, irresponsibly, or with hurtful intent, then love—or its counterfeit, coercive power—can lead to harm and even death. Too often, lust is mistaken for love, which in turn becomes the rationale for selfish behaviors. When infatuation, lust, and self-gratification take the place of the responsibilities of love, cascading consequences result that can be devastating for partners, children, families, and society.

In recognizing the many ways in which people misuse power and love, we need to be honest about sin and the finite limitations of human beings.

Children and youth live in a highly sexualized world. They are exposed early to patterns of adult sexuality and are pressured to associate their bodies with practices that devalue them. Examples include child beauty contests, sexually suggestive clothing, sexually charged prime time, cable television programs, and movies. At an early age, children listen to sexualized music that is deliberately marketed to them. They "date" as couples and engage in genital activity at earlier ages. Children and youth are targets of sexual bullying, destructive language, and vicious humor.

The ELCA regards the overexposure of emotionally maturing children and teens to adult sexuality as a failure on the part of adults and society. It challenges all individuals and institutions in society to fulfill their responsibility to protect and nurture children and youth and provide for their appropriate development. Congregations should offer opportunities for adults to express these concerns and explore solutions together.

Expanding cyberspace and other electronic media create new challenges to the protection of children and youth. It is important that parents, society, and lawmakers continue to be extremely vigilant to protect the well-being of children and youth in this electronic world with its often hidden dangers. The widespread electronic availability of violent and degrading pornography threatens children and youth, as well as adults. It has the capacity to damage the normal sexual development in those who view it, often obsessively and in secret. How to address this problem is one of the most important child-protection issues of our time, and our church will be an active participant in this important conversation.

The sexual education of children and teens will be supported as a priority by this church. Anecdotal evidence among teens suggests that few parents or congregations meaningfully engage young people in either sex education or healthy conversations about sexuality, even though teens would welcome it. This lack of engagement is remarkable, especially considering the associated dangers. This church will give particular attention to how children and youth are supported, nurtured, and accompanied in their sexual and relational formation. Toward that end, this church reaffirms what it has said previously about providing comprehensive sex education within the context of Christian faith. This education must begin early and emphasize responsibility and mutuality. Such education should focus on sustaining conversation about what is good and what is harmful in ways appropriate to growing maturity levels. It should avoid simply requiring compliance with approved or rejected behaviors but should emphasize the exploration of why certain behaviors are rejected because they are damaging, why and how some pressures should be resisted, and what differentiates mature and rewarding sexual love from exploitative and demeaning forms.

We are sexual beings from the beginning of our lives. The ancient psalmist envisioned the divine mystery of our embodied lives long before science investigated our biological and genetic complexity. "For it was you who formed my inward parts; you knit me together in my mother's womb" (Psalm 139:13). The realities of our sexual bodies are visible in physical features and powerful in less visible characteristics.

This means much more than that we are born with male, female, or sometimes with ambiguous genitalia. Our cells carry sex chromosomes, and our endocrine systems infuse our bodies with hormones. In ways that are still not fully understood, we develop strong gender identities at a very early age. While there is still much to be learned about the biological complexity of human beings, we have come to understand that this complexity suggests a variety of sexual orientations and gender identities.

We all have sexual identities that will find expression in our lives. We have sexual feelings that we are aware of and sometimes need to be negotiated when we are interacting with friends, courting a potential life partner, working closely with colleagues, or sharing our lives with another. Moreover, we must evaluate and respond constantly to the ways in which the sexuality of others is expressed. We must respond to sexual stimuli in the environment, including the varieties of human touch, which may vary from casual contact through flirtatious appreciation to invitations to intense physical intimacy.

A healthy sense of sexuality is related to having a healthy body image. This church teaches that caring for the body and following practices that lead to physical and emotional wellness are part of the stewardship of created goodness. It recognizes that a positive sense of one's own body supports a healthy sense of one's gender identity and sexuality.

Sometimes, it can be very hard to develop and maintain positive attitudes about one's body. Too many people struggle for a healthy sense of body as a result of experiences of degradation or shaming by others, including family members and intimate partners. This church will support all in affirming and reclaiming a sense of healthy sexuality.

This church calls attention to the danger of embracing standards of physical attractiveness that exclude many, including the aged and people with disabilities, and which distort the understanding of what it means to be healthy. The young whose bodies are changing and growing may be especially vulnerable to idealized and commercialized images of a "perfect body" that play on insecurities and destructive self-loathing.

A holistic understanding of the interrelationship of body, mind, and spirit challenges such narrow understandings of beauty. It enables us better to affirm the many dimensions of beauty and to celebrate human variety and particularity.

Couples—whether teenage, young adult, mature, or senior—move from a first acquaintance into a journey of increasing knowledge, appreciation, and trust in each other. This journey involves spiritual, emotional, intellectual, and physical dimensions of self-understanding. When these dimensions develop at similar rates, trust and entrusting are established and secured. When they are out of balance, trust may either not exist or disintegrate.

Care must be taken in sex education materials and processes to inform about the dangers of diseases without teaching that sexual expression is intrinsically dirty and dangerous. Efforts emphasize responsibility and mutuality. Such education should focus on sustaining conversation about what is good and what is harmful in ways appropriate to growing maturity levels. It should avoid simply requiring compliance with approved or rejected behaviors but should emphasize the exploration of why certain behaviors are rejected because they are damaging, why and how some pressures should be resisted, and what differentiates mature and rewarding sexual love from exploitative and demeaning forms.

Efforts at public education and protection from disease should be supported. This includes efforts that challenge stigma and discrimination, especially against those living with and affected by HIV and AIDS. This church, including its institutions and agencies, should be an active partner in discussions about how to address and contain epidemics of such diseases.

The Evangelical Lutheran Church has taken the time in going extensively into the subject matter of sexuality, and I believe they have included all areas of this subject from a physical and scriptural bases. This is only a small embodiment of their belief on the subject, so please take the time to research their site for more information.

Puberty is setting in earlier in our children than thirty or forty years ago, and if society is still haggling over this situation of sexuality, we are going to have some very serious problems more than only pregnancy, necking, and kissing to contend with. The headline below speaks for itself on this reasoning. Whatever the reason for this situation, the fact is that our children are developing (maturing) earlier and earlier.

Doctors Planning to Use Depo-Provera to Combat Early Puberty in Children

Submitted by Dasha on November 1, 2012

A new study released by the American Academy of Pediatrics states that boys in America are reaching puberty at an earlier age than is considered standard thirty to forty years ago, which translates to a full six months to two years earlier than the medical community has previously acknowledged as normal. Marcia Herman-Giddens, lead author and adjunct professor of maternal and child health for the University of North Carolina School of Global Public Health (GPH), states that this comprehensive study identified the age that boys are forming enlarged testes, which directly correlates to their sperm production and found that

- African-American boys hit puberty on average by nine years old,
- Caucasian boys hit puberty on average by ten years old, and
- Hispanic boys hit puberty on average by ten years old.

Herman-Giddens says that "this should have an impact on the public health community." Per the research, Herman-Giddens claims that environment is causing these fast changes in young males' development. "Genetics take maybe hundreds, thousands of years. You have to look at something in the environment. That would include everything from (a lack of) exercise to junk food to TV to chemicals."

Previous studies have linked chemical exposure to decreases in sperm production, birth defects, and behavioral problems in children. However, this study is devoid of information as to what the mechanism by which this phenomenon is occurring; the differences in racial genetics; and the exposure to chemicals in food, water, and environment that could contribute to early puberty in boys.

The GPH are dedicated to using science to combat global issues, such as global health, diabetes, obesity, access to clean water, and global mental health.

Being a globalist organization, they use students and UNC faculty to pinpoint strategic planning efforts in order to have the most impact and influence on public health problems. They have at their disposal the Gillings Innovation Labs, which is funded by private-sector donors to facilitate genetic engineering solutions to natural biochemical issues.

Sonya Lunder, senior analyst for the Environmental Working Group (EWG), explains that "it's a very complicated subject. We're finding a lot of the chemicals that Americans have daily exposure to have an impact." Lunder believes that identifying specific chemicals in our food and environment, like bisphenol A (BPA), as the causation of this new development is difficult to do. She is more concerned about the "shortening childhood" than the impact this physiological change will have on our future fertility rates and the chemical alteration of young males' brains.

In 2010, a study was released describing the early pubescent development of girls in the US. At the age of seven, girls are now experiencing a disturbing biochemical change. Simultaneously, they are being exposed to sex education in schools before they are able to properly process the information.

BPA was virtually ignored as a probable cause for this new trend. BPA is a highly toxic estrogen accelerator that is used in all plastic products commercially produced. The chemical mimics natural estrogen when leeched into the body. It offsets natural estrogen levels, causing the body to hasten its pubescent generation. Nearly all children are exposed to this chemical through plastic toys, pacifiers, bottles, and sippy cups. Its influence on natural hormone distribution within the body has proven to be incredibly damaging.

Girls are finding they are coming into puberty earlier and earlier.

Boys are showing retardation of their sexual anatomy, halting their pubescent maturity.

As our children enter adulthood, these hormonal imbalances cause breast cancer. Because of the lack of mainstream information concerning this chemical, the connection between this trend and BPA is dismissed. The effects of BPA are cumulative and therefore not readily connected as the causation of early pubescent development.

The EWG are a nonprofit organization that uses the "power of public information to protect public health and the environment." They are essentially a nongovernmental organization (NGO) working to "replace federal policies with policies that invest in conservation and sustainable development." Through lobby tactics on Capitol Hill, they use federal-grant money to go up against those organizations and elected representatives that do not subscribe to their goals.

The EWG receives funding from ecofascist organizations, such as the 11th Hour Project and the Wallace Global Fund; pharmaceutical corporations, like

Johnson Family Foundation and John Merck Fund; and globalists, like the Turner Foundation and Civil Society Institute.

Herman-Giddens recommends that parents keep a close watch on their children for signs of depression, poor self-esteem, and eating disorders as a result of early puberty. The collaboration of the pharmaceutical industry with these early pubescent boys may be an answer worth investigating, according to these researchers. She states, "The problem is that as a culture we are encouraging a longer and longer adolescence. We're delaying maturity in our culture, by staying longer in school, being later to leave the parent's home, later to marry, later to get financial security. And that means that we have now a huge discrepancy between when the body starts to mature physically and when overall maturity is achieved, which may mean that a boy's or girl's cognitive and social skills do not necessarily mature earlier just because the body does. So, there may be a big and growing gap here, which can cause all sorts of concern for guidance and teaching."

Girls are finding they are coming into puberty earlier and earlier.

Because of these new findings, study researchers are suggesting that boys be exposed to sexual ideals because of their early pubescent development. Herman-Giddens says that by third grade, parents need to have sex talks with children. Boys will want to have sex earlier, and candid talks with children about sex may avoid confusion and situations where they act out sexually.

Central precocious puberty (CPP) is a new medical condition that coincides with studies like the one published by Herman-Giddens. CPP is defined as "a condition where puberty starts too soon in children—usually in girls under eight years old and boys under nine years old." When the brain of a child releases hormones from the adrenal glands or pituitary gland too early, premature onset of pubescent emergence is manifested, which affects the central nervous system, as well as the developing brain.

These are interesting information but frightening. Our youths are maturing earlier, but their cognitive and social skill delays, while boys will want to have sex earlier. These are our future men and women; this is a dismal situation. As adults (churches and government), where are we in this fight? As I write, several songs come to mind. But this stood out, and this is the "Greatest Love of All." It says that the children are our future and we are to teach them well so they can lead the way, but in order for them to do that, we need to show them the beauty they possess inside, which will give them a sense of pride. For the writer writes that he found the greatest love inside (where does God reside? In the heart).

I am not sure what mind-set the writer had in mind when he wrote "so I learn to depend on me" because learning to love oneself is the greatest love of all.

What should one take away from this song? It can go one way or another depending on the individual's view, but the hope will be that the individual will see the beauty of God through and through, knowing that there is greatness waiting to explore spiritually and not carnally.

The greatest love—1 Corinthians 13:4–8 (KJV) states that love is long-suffering and kind. It does not envy, does not parade itself, is not puffed up, does not behave rudely, does not seek its own, is not provoked, thinks no evil, does not rejoice in iniquity but rejoice in the truth, bears all things, believe all things, hopes all things, and endures all things. <u>Love never fails</u>.

Many have listened to this song over and over again and enjoyed it. But how much do we believe that they are our future, and how do they (our children) understand that they have the greatest love of all? What does that mean to them when they feel betrayed by circumstances beyond their control of which they cannot understand? Can they really love themselves? I remember turning to my church at a time when I was going through distress because I was behind in my rent, and after speaking to the pastor, I was told that the board of the church would not be able to help me because my name was not on the books as a member of that particular branch of the church even though I had been attending for many years and had been paying into the church budget. How many have turned to the churches and was spurned or sexually abused? I also remember while working at a group home for girls and speaking to a young lady who was brought there because she was on the streets for a long time and was now pregnant by her boyfriend (who also lived on the street) and turned herself in to social services to get help. I had an opportunity to speak with this young lady several times because I could seriously feel her pain. She thought nothing of herself and consistently called herself a whore, and when I asked her why she did that, she said because her mother was a whore and so she considers herself a whore also. It so happens that on the day I did not work, this same young lady, out of anguish, thrust her hand fully through the closed glass window, cutting herself through her arm. The ambulance was called, and she was taken to the hospital. Some came from rough neighborhoods, and some came from well-to-do homes. And one wonders what is missing. Where is the missing link? Kirk Franklin wrote this:

This is for that little child with no
father
For that man that doesn't have a place to stay
And for that little boy living with
AIDS
Can I tell you a story, tell you a
story?
You can lean on me

There are too many youths who are saying "Where is He?" or "How can I feel Him of whom I do not know?" I want that shoulder to lean on. Matthew 25:40 says, "Inasmuch as ye have done it unto one of the least of these brethren, ye have done it unto me."

This is the song that most will sing:

> Well, they tell me of a pie up in the sky, waiting for me when I die. But between the day you're born and when you die, they never seem to hear even your cry. So as sure as the sun will shine, I'm gonna get my share right now what's mine because the harder they come, the harder they fall one and all.

Even with things looking so dismal, there are still those who are reaching out and making a difference, and I will quote the Oprah Winfrey Network. I particularly like the spiritual journey that she is taking, and hopefully one day, her network will embark upon this difficult subject of teaching fornication through a biblical tone. There are so many books and CDs on spiritual lessons and blessings, but I am yet to hear or see one that touches the subject in this way. One of the CDs that touched my heart was the *Secret* written by Rhonda Byrne in the Law of Attraction, essentially what you think of you attract. The CD of the *Secret* has filled in a large gap of my journey as I absorb it into my thought, feeding it into my being. I would love a copy of these CDs to get into the hands of as many teens, if not all, if nothing else but for encouragement. It speaks that there is no lack, and I believe this to be true. But tell this to the youth who lives for today and have no vision of being better for today or the mom who has a couple of kids and no father around to embrace them with love and teach them sound doctrine and what is considered morals and integrity. Many fathers out there are youth themselves, and this only complicates matters worse, for they are in much need of spiritual guidance themselves.

As I started off saying our greatest problem today is of a sexual nature, it is nothing new. It has only been extended to incorporate our young more than ever because so much is now open to them. Sex is a responsible action, and many of our youths have no concept of this responsibility. They have opened Pandora's box, which they cannot close easily.

There is nothing new to this subject; it is as old as one can think of, but the subject matter doesn't get any easier to speak about. Many greats have fallen in this category—kings, presidents, or men of high positions right down to this time. Paul the Apostle calls it a burning, and it certainly is a man after God's own heart. King David did not realize that he had fallen in the trap to where he put a man to death to cover his sin of sleeping with Bathsheba (Uriah's wife). Solomon (David's son), who was supposed to be the wisest man ever lived, had over five hundred wives and so many concubines. Due to this situation, his mind wandered away from what God wanted as he was led astray to do those things, which was an abomination. And even with so many examples, nations are still committing the same mistakes over and over again. Just about every child is taught about David and Bathsheba, Solomon and Sheba, and Samson and Delilah. But have they been taught the true cause of each act and of the punishment that followed each? We need to once again revisit the Word of the living God in raising our children. We cannot continue to stand hiding behind the government to teach our children right from wrong. So many programs have been cut due to economic constraints that many of our youths don't have much options anymore.

My heart and soul groan for the youth of this century, for the lack is great, yet we live in so much wealth of information. I became a business partner with several wonderful people a couple of years ago (not affiliated now), and I have gone to many seminars and listen to many great speakers. And in each, one thing they all have in common is they speak of having time with family. Some speak of taking their children back and forth to school, which is wonderful, as I had that done for my second daughter also. I was beyond happy as I had to pull her out of one school because in my mind, I had to save my child from the influence of the friends she was around, so I am not putting down those who are able to do this but mentioned to say that it would be nice if there was some form of unity for all children to afford this type of living. Some speak of taking their children to great locations in the world on vacation, but even in all this, I think of one thing: are they also teaching their children about being there for their friends who may or may not live in the same neighborhood or speak the same way they do or have a different dress code?

Yes, we all want the best for our children, but how about teaching them about loving their neighbor and who their neighbor is? I remember having an experience with one of my youngest daughter's friend's mom. Each morning my daughter would go next door to walk with her friend to the bus stop and take the bus to go to school, and this one morning my daughter ran back to me crying because her friend's mother told her she should not come back to her house and she could not play with her daughter anymore because my daughter was telling her daughter about sexual things. I calmed my daughter down and went next door to find out what happened, and as I knocked on the door next door, the woman screamed without opening the door, "Get off my property, and if you don't leave, I will call the police!" I left and went back to my house. A day later, I received a call from social service that someone had reported that I was leaving my child, who was about seven or eight years old at the time, alone. I had a very good idea who made that call, but I left it alone. There was a follow-up from the social service to prove no such thing. This is only one instance of what we sometimes teach our children of neighborly love. In this instance though, I believe that there was more to it than two children speaking on sexual matters. What was this mother so afraid of that she could not come to me about my daughter if she was so concerned about what was said between her daughter and my daughter? A few years later, that family moved away, but I was told that they returned to the area a year or two later. Now how do I know this? I know of this because my daughter, who the mother chased from her doorstep, told me so. This is to say, these two girls remain friends in spite of that incident.

Many are taught to go to school and become educated and get a job. Yes, we want our children educated, but after the education, then what? It's not about truly doing for their neighbors because of love but out of ambition. The truth is no matter the position of our children, those that are given much (privilege) are never better than those without because they are either facing or fighting the same battle of sexual desires. We need not look too far for "Hollywood." As I have said previously, the soap opera taught me how to cheat, steal, or fall in love with a fool. It is doing the same job continuously. I sometimes wonder if this is the reason for the common assault of divorce in the celebrity world and why it is so rampant.

Pain is not biased; it shows no favoritism and does not discriminate. I learned early that when you cross the line of integrity, there is always a price to pay. It is only a matter of time. We are experiencing it now, looking at our government and churches. "God is no respecter of person," Lisa Nichols says on the CD of the secret that there is a delay in what we think, while Paul puts it this way, "All things are not expedient, and I mean it in the sense of urgency. And thank God that while we do things in hiding, He who is our Creator always gives us enough time to retreat and rethink and repent." I quote the song of Jimmy Cliff (a musician) because there are many Jimmy Cliffs out there; and unfortunately, I would say there are more of them than other groups. They are in the ghettos "hood" in privilege homes and in corporate, but for the ones who did not see the movie *The Harder They Come*, the character Jimmy Cliff died in the end, as he came out shooting while riddled with bullets from all directions by government agents.

Condoleezza Rice had made a statement that is quite true, for she said, "Your greatest ally in controlling your response to your circumstance is in a quality education," because she can look at a zip code and can tell whether one is going to get a good education or not. But should it really matter where you come from? It matters where you are going. As one young woman said in a Facebook message, "I am not what happened to me. I am what I choose to become." There is much truth to this statement, but tell that to a young child of twelve or twenty-three years of age who is already a murderer or a thief and is locked up. One can only know this truth when they have been given the tools at an early age. The crisis in the K-12 education is a threat to the very fabric of who we are. If she said nothing else for the rest of her life, this statement sums up everything in a nutshell. She speaks well. She speaks from the aspect of learning math, English, or science.

But I speak from the viewpoint of adding spiritual things into the mix because not every child is drawn to learning math, English, or science—but all are drawn or faced with sex at one time or another. This is guaranteed.

Teach the children, and teach them well. Give them something to believe in, for they are the future of the world, and what we put in is what we will get out. Educate the parents, and open up adequate programs to allow them to be viable participants in their children's lives. If parents are to be more involved in their children's lives, as the survey reports, then there needs to be more commitment on the part of our religious institutions to accommodate and spearhead this direction. This is going to take much sanctification and purification on the part of the church leaders because so much damage has already been done by the church that much hope in the church has been lost. God's hand is still not too short that it cannot accommodate our needs nor His will to cleanse us again unto righteousness.

The Gift

Who doesn't love gifts? Pretty much everyone wants it. I am big on gifts, especially getting them. How many of us receive a gift and turn around and discard it in the trash or, if we lose it, we are not remorseful?

The human race was given not one but two gifts more precious than any other gift—a gift of HIS death on the cross and procreation (the ability to multiply). What do we do with these gifts? We throw them aside and abuse our bodies in any way we wish. The holidays will soon be upon us, and most are expecting gifts from loved ones and special people, but that special gift that can never be bought or sold is ignored.

As I have said before, the government has been doing their part in putting money through various channels in regard to this situation and our youths. Looking at the surveys done for each state, it's interesting that in each, the solution is the same—better health education, more comprehensive health services, more supportive policies, and more family involvement. All are important. I will end by saying we need a different strategy in educating our youths because from where many stand, what they are seeing are contradictions—do what I say but not what I do. It's unfortunate to say, but like most not just our youths, the song sung by Johnny Lee sums it up beautifully. "Some spend a lifetime looking for love in all the wrong places, looking into too many wrong faces, searching eyes, looking for traces of what they hope to find and dream of, hoping to find a friend." I especially love this area: playing a fool's game never to win. Just as we think highly of sexual intercourse, such is the same as spiritual fornication.

Again, as before, this book is not written to judge or blast anyone over the head with brimstone and fire. But if we are true to ourselves, in examining ourselves, we will find ourselves fitting nicely in the pages of this book. If this stands true, then where do we fit in the scheme of life in how to assist in the fight of spiritual enlightenment to our young adults coming into the future? I do not expect some will ever care about what's written in this book as they will find excuses not to care, but I know many will.

As it was said by one minister of God, Pastor Alistair Begg, we will never be satisfied in God until He is gloried in us. The work was not done in Christ Jesus until the Father was completely glorified in His Son, for what is the chief end of man but to glorify God and to enjoy Him forever.

We are thirsty people, but we keep trying to quench that thirst with material things. In the end, we will go back to exactly what Solomon said in Ecclesiastes, "Let us the conclusion of the whole matter, fear God, and keep His commandments, for this is the whole duty of man." What else did he say (there goes that word again)? "Remember, now thy Creator in the days of thy [what?] youth." How many of us heard it said that when someone is dying, they speak that they should have spent more time in the office or asked for their precious ornament(s)? What a sad going-away present. A message to all: Do not shut yourselves up to yourselves, satisfied to pour out all your affection upon each other. Seize every opportunity to contribute to the happiness of those around you, sharing with them your affection. Words of kindness, looks of sympathy, and expressions of appreciation would—to many a struggling, lonely one—be a cup of cold water to a thirsty soul. A word of cheer, an act of kindness, would go far to lighten the burdens that are resting heavily upon weary shoulders. It is in unselfish ministry that true happiness is found (*Testimonies for the Church* vol. 7, 50).

Christ died that the life of man might be bound up with His life in the union of divinity and humanity. Live in the sunshine of the Savior's love, and then your influence will bless the world. Let the Spirit of Christ control you. Let the kindness be ever on your lips. Forbearance and unselfishness mark the words and actions of those who are born again, to live the new life in Christ.

Printed in the United States
By Bookmasters